The Pontop & South Shields Railway

ROB LANGHAM

AMBERLEY

First published 2024

Amberley Publishing
The Hill, Stroud,
Gloucestershire, GL5 4EP

www.amberley-books.com

ISBN: 978 1 3981 1461 6 (print)
ISBN: 978 1 3981 1462 3 (ebook)

British Library Cataloguing in Publication Data.
A catalogue record for this book is available from the British Library.

Typeset in 10pt on 13pt Celeste.
Origination by Amberley Publishing.
Printed in the UK.

Contents

CHAPTER 1

Beginnings

In 1841, the Pontop & South Shields Railway was formed. Unlike most others being set up at the time, the Pontop & South Shields Railway (P&SSR) was not formed to build a railway, but to take over an existing one, the Stanhope & Tyne which ran for over 30 miles from limestone quarries at Crawleyside, to the north of Stanhope, a market town in Weardale in County Durham, and running in a roughly north-easterly direction across County Durham to a set of eight large coal drops on the River Tyne at South Shields. The speed at which the Pontop & South Shields Railway was formed, continuing the operation of the eastern half of the Stanhope & Tyne Railroad Company's line from South Shields to Carr House following its dissolution in early 1841, serves as a strong indicator for how successful that part of the railway was. Although the Stanhope & Tyne Railroad Company (S&TR) folded owing to its severe debts accrued in the construction of the line, lack of traffic on the western half of the line and hampered by the ongoing cost of wayleaves paid to cross landowners' property, the movement of coal on the eastern half of the line was large enough to warrant its takeover and continued operation by the new company, formed by twenty-five of the original forty-nine major shareholders of the S&TR.

The history of the S&TR is detailed in *The Stanhope & Tyne Railroad Company* (Fonthill Media, 2020), while the later history of the western half, which after closure from 1839 was bought from the P&SSR and reopened in 1842 by the Derwent Iron Company and then taken over by the Stockton & Darlington Railway in 1845, is covered in *The Wear & Derwent Railway* (Fonthill Media, 2022). This book does the same for the Pontop & South Shields Railway. To cover the history of this line in more detail, it is necessary to give an overview of its earlier history in S&TR ownership to set the scene.

Formed as a company in 1831, the S&TR started to arrange wayleaves for the line to cross landowners' property and leases to mine coal. The section that became the Pontop & South Shields Railway, between Carr House/Leadgate and South Shields, proved to be the most profitable in the early years owing to the amount of coal to be mined and transported out of the area. The S&TR was not the first railway in the area, as wooden waggonways had existed for over a century prior to the 1830s, taking coal from pits across County Durham and especially in the Pontop area of North West Durham around Stanley and Tanfield down to the rivers Tyne and Wear. By the time the S&TR was created, over 22 million

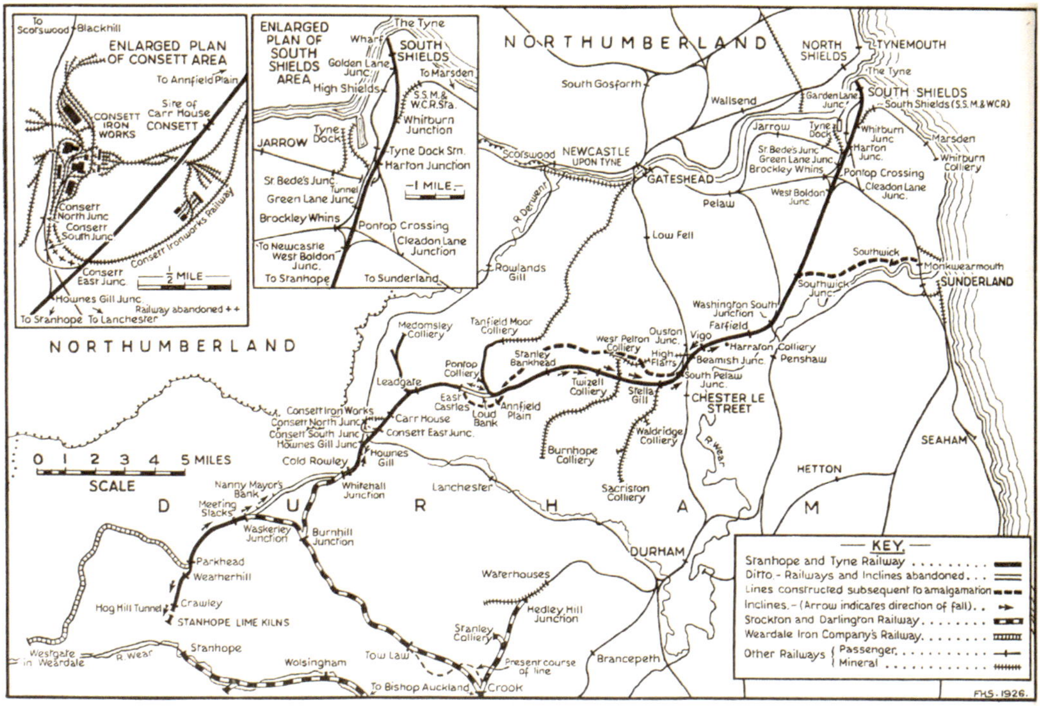

MAP OF THE STANHOPE AND TYNE RY.

Map showing the Pontop & South Shields Railway route, its deviations, and links with other lines in 1926. The Pontop & South Shields Railway itself ran from South Shields to Carr House (Leadgate) on the original Stanhope & Tyne, with the Derwent Iron Company and then Stockton & Darlington Railway taking over the route westward of here, although it became part of the same company again in 1863 when the Stockton & Darlington Railway was acquired by the North Eastern Railway.

tons of coal was being mined a year nationwide – double that of 1800. The previously horse-worked winding engines or 'gins' that worked relatively close to the surface pits were being replaced by steam-powered winding engines, allowing pits to be worked deeper and more productively; steam engines also pumped water out of deep pits to access previously inaccessible seams. As the coal trade increased, so too did the need for more shipping points.

Initially there were plans for the S&TR to head north along the Derwent Valley from the Consett area to reach the Tyne, but it was instead decided to head towards South Shields where coal could be loaded directly into seagoing ships rather than into a keel boat and then transhipped at the mouth of the Tyne. The South Shields route did originally look at adopting the Beamish Waggonway, which had recently been re-laid with iron rails, but this did not come to fruition. Annfield House, dating back to the eighteenth century and still standing at the top of Loud Hill in Annfield Plain, was used as offices, with resident engineer Thomas Elliot Harrison giving it as the correspondence address for an advert for contractors for 'formation of cuts and embankments' for the line between Hownes Gill and Pontop in September 1832.[1] The consulting engineer for the line was Robert Stephenson,

Portrait of Thomas Elliot Harrison in later life.

who was heavily preoccupied at this time with construction of the London & Birmingham Railway which Harrison had worked under Stephenson on. Annfield House was ideally located, roughly midway between the S&TR's route between Crawleyside, Stanhope and South Shields. Annfield House remained in the use of the S&TR for some years; in 1837 it was described as 'their central station' during a report of the former resident agent for the S&TR, John Grainger, being presented with a 'very handsome silver snuff box' on his leaving of the company.[2] In late 1837, and again in 1838, Annfield House's estate is described as 'all in the occupation of the Stanhope and Tyne Railway Company' which included the house itself, outbuildings, and three other dwelling houses (although two of these were tenanted by others) together with 13 acres of plantations.[3,4] It is not known if the house remained occupied after it was sold – if it was – by the S&TR or any of the railway companies that followed it.

In May 1833 tenders were requested by the directors of the S&TR for 2,000 tons of malleable iron rails, 500lbs worth of around £30 to the yard and the remaining 1,500 tons at £40 to the yard 'of the form usually denominated "fish bellied"' and made of the best iron together with 'a suitable quantity of CAST IRON CHAIRS weighing about 10 and 15lb. each, and the necessary Wrought Iron KEYS and PINS for the same'.[5] Construction of the railway also required the building of a quayside dock at South Shields where the three (later increased to five, then eight) enormous coal drops lowered full chaldrons (coal wagons) over the holds of collier ships for unloading. This was the scene of a 'melancholy and fatal accident' in January 1834 when a young man called John Stodd was dressing stones underneath a pile of large stones when the top gave way. Two of these stones 'about 4 tons each, fell upon him, and literally crushed him to pieces'.[6]

On 28 March 1834, there was an advert 'To Plate-Layers' in the *Durham Chronicle*: 'Twenty good HANDS may have immediate Employment in LAYING the PERMANENT ROADS

The S&TR's 'central station' at Annfield House on Loud Bank, built some time before 1778 and close to the stationary engine that worked the inclined plane on each side of the bank. The house still stands today. (Beamish Museum)

upon the Stanhope and Tyne Railroad.' Applicants were to write to Richard Parr, contractor for construction of the eastern end of the railway. The same notice advertised that Parr was looking to hire or purchase two steam locomotives, either new or second hand.[7]

The western half of the line from Stanhope to Annfield Plain opened on 15 May 1834, the day starting with a 'party of gentlemen' leaving 'Annfield at eight o'clock in the morning, by a railway wagon tastefully fitted up for the occasion, and arrived at the termination of the line about eleven, highly gratified with the whole line of road, but especially with that part of it which crosses the precipitous ravine called the Hownes'.[8] The day was later marked by the runaway of four wagons down the Weatherhill incline, killing three.

The eastern half of the line from Annfield to South Shields opened four months later, on 10 September 1834. To mark the opening:

> Rejoicings and ceremonies commenced at day-break, by the discharge of a great number of carronades, placed on the banks of the Tyne and on the heights in the Neighbourhood. At the same time a merry tune pealed from the bells of the parish church, and the Company's locomotive engines started for Medomsley, to bring down the hundred wagons of Medomsley coals intended for shipment.
>
> At an early hour the appearances in the town gave evidence of the deep interest felt in the success of this great undertaking by the inhabitants. Business was suspended and the shops were closed. Flags and banners, bearing appropriate inscriptions, waved from the windows of the inns, and also from many private houses. The inscriptions and decorations generally had reference to the railway; and we only noticed one flag of a political tendency. It was inscribed 'Earl Grey and No Revolution'.

Left: Robert Stephenson, 1835. (George Richmond)

Below: The Stanhope & Tyne Hotel in Annfield Plain, built adjacent to the line with a brewery at the rear. It was built in 1835 and run by Charles Allen, who was a contractor to the S&TR for making cuttings and embankments. Unfortunately, in recent years it was destroyed by fire. (Beamish Museum)

Dignitaries 'proceeded on the railway, in a handsome car' at one o'clock in the afternoon, including Thomas Elliot Harrison, John Fairweather Harrison (Thomas Elliot Harrison's uncle), A. J. F. Marreco, two of the London directors, and William Harrison (Thomas Elliot Harrison's father), the managing director. Noticeably, Robert Stephenson was not present, likely busy with other concerns. This was pulled by a 'small engine' which another 'party of gentlemen' climbed onto. This 'small engine' and 'handsome car' returned to South Shields with the other locomotives and their trains of loaded wagons for loading the coal onto the brig *Sally* which itself had 'her masts and rigging literally covered with flags of all colours and descriptions'. Despite the 'almost incessant rain' which by this point had gone on for two hours, it did not 'damp the ardour of the people' who in large numbers enjoyed the spectacle together with the band, a royal salute being fired from the *Northumberland* and the firing of carronades. One of the many flags on display was of blue silk, inscribed with 'Harrison and Company, and Humanity', paid for by 'the numerous work-people, who took this method of evincing their gratitude to the Proprietors, for their very liberal conduct during the progress of the work. In all cases where medical aid was required, it had been promptly provided at the expence of the company; and in those very few instances where accidents have occurred, the wife and family of the sufferer, (if he had any) have been supported'.

The 1834 Coal and Lime Landsale Depot from West Boldon, relocated to Beamish Museum and reduced in size from six 'cells' to four.

Following the shipment of the coals, the thousand or so men employed on the S&TR were 'regaled with a substantial dinner' at pubs across South Shields, paid for by the company. During the construction, the S&TR had spent around £1,000 per week in wages alone, giving an indication of the incredible cost the S&TR had incurred in building the line.[9]

The railway's main line was of 33¾ miles in length, 17 miles of which, at the eastern end, were double track. The eastern half, the half that was continued to be worked by the Pontop & South Shields Railway, originated at the foot of the eastern side of Carr House incline, which was worked by a stationary engine that worked the incline up its western side from Hownes Gill. Although the line originated at Crawleyside, near Stanhope, at the great limestone quarries and limekilns built by the S&TR, there was minimal mineral or other resources until the railway reached this point east of Carr House. Here, however, was the extensive coalfield at Lanchester Common, where the S&TR had two collieries open at Pontop and Medomsley (which was reached by a 1½-mile-long branch from the main line) before the railway had opened. As the railway headed east towards South Shields, it passed close to other collieries and through the extensive coalfield awaiting to be opened. The line from South Shields to Annfield, nearly 19 miles long, had been built in fifteen months.

From the foot of the Carr House east inclined plane, moving eastward towards South Shields as the loaded traffic would in the 'chaldron' wagons (holding a unit of measurement known as the 'Newcastle chaldron' – 53cwt or just over 2½ tons of coal), travel along the 2¼-mile-long level section through the village of Leadgate to Bantling Castle, known as the Medomsley Level, which was worked by horse haulage. At Bantling Castle, the foot of an inclined plane was reached. Here, in the shadow of Pontop Pike, a stationary engine pulled wagons up the Annfield West inclined plane of 662 yards, then down Annfield East inclined plane of 1,056 yards. The east side of the hill (Loud Hill) is known as Loud Bank, with the railway running on the north side of what is now West Road. The inclined plane changed the name of the settlement it ran through: Annfield had 'Plane' added to its name, later changing to 'Plain', which it is still called. Annfield House is down a short track from West Road, at the junction of which stood the Annfield incline engine.

At the foot of the Annfield East incline, the line was level enough for horses to work the Stanley Level through to West Stanley. It was joined here by a branch just over 2 miles long to Tanfield Moor pit, part of which was re-laid over the older Harelaw Waggonway. Coming to the edge of a significant ridge, to descend over 400 feet in a few miles, there were a series of self-acting inclined planes, which were known as the Pontop inclines. Using the heavier, loaded wagons of coal going downhill to pull up lighter (usually empty) wagons via a rope around a brake wheel at the head of the incline, this was a highly efficient way of moving wagons downhill. These were common in the North East, where moving coal from uphill areas down to the coast or river meant the gradient was in favour of the traffic. The operation of the self-acting inclines is described more fully in a later chapter, but in essence they were operated by a brakesman at the head of the incline operating a brake wheel, with the set of wagons each having a bankrider travelling with them to take the rope off when they finished their journey – or in an emergency. A simple, effective form of signalling existed along the inclines called a 'token wire' which ran just above the ground alongside the inclines, which made both a visual and audible signal at each end of the incline.

The 1835 S&TR limekilns at Bantling Castle, near Annfield Plain, described in 1844 as 'capable of supplying from 5 to 6 Wagons of Clot lime per day'.

Above: A close-up of the titling on the limekilns.

Below: Tanfield Moor pit, served by the S&TR until its traffic was 'won' by the Brandling Railway on their takeover of the Tanfield Waggonway. (Beamish Museum)

The first inclined plane was Stanley incline at 1,276 yards, followed immediately by Twizell at 880 yards, then Eden Hill at 1,122 yards. The Pelton Level at 1,331 yards was worked by horses before the Waldridge incline. Stanley and Twizell inclines were, at some point, combined, and in 1923 the incline lengths and gradients were given as Stanley incline at 2,048 yards long (although in 1898 the Chief Engineer of the North Eastern Railway gave its length as 2,250 yards with a rope 2,300 yards long) with an average gradient of 1 in 27, Eden Hill 1,089 yards long with an average gradient of 1 in 22, and Waldridge 957 yards long with an average gradient of 1 in 23.

Stella Gill, at the foot of Waldridge incline, became a large marshalling yard for the traffic going up and down the Pontop inclines. There was a level section for ¾ of a mile which was worked by a stationary engine at High Flatts using a tail rope. The High Flatts engine also worked the incline, which ran downhill for ¾ of a mile eastwards from it towards the Great North Road, or Durham Turnpike Road, at Birtley. The railway originally crossed the road, which is now the A167, on the level. At the Great North Road the line went significantly uphill for the first time since Loud Bank or Annfield West incline, with the engine at Vigo pulling wagons up the west side then lowering them down the east side to Biddick Burn, where the railway was crossed over the burn by the large wooden bridge known as Fatfield Gears over the cutting, later culverted and turned into a large earth embankment.

Here began the locomotive-worked section of the line, where powerful 0-4-2 and later 0-6-0 Large Samson locomotives designed by Robert Stephenson worked the traffic towards

Side profile of a Stanhope & Tyne 0-4-2 Large Samson locomotive without its tender.

South Shields. There was 9¼ miles of practically level railway running north-eastwards through what is now the built-up area of Washington but at the time was sparsely populated, and close to West Boldon before crossing the River Don at Brockley Whins. The railway ran at 15 feet above street level through South Shields at the insistence of the local improvement commission, with the locomotive works and wagon workshop to the north of King Street. Wagons were marshalled here before being taken down to the riverside drops on the west side of South Shields on the River Tyne.

Use of inclined planes was common at this time and had plenty of advantages, but it had disadvantages too. Whereas if a locomotive failed there were others that could do the work, something going wrong on an incline could cause severe disruption; for example, in late October 1837 when damage to the main shaft of the Vigo engine caused operations on the line to be partially suspended for just over a week until repairs could be effected.[10]

Traffic on the eastern half of the Stanhope & Tyne showed promise. Even the lime trade, which soon became a financial millstone around the neck of the company, showed enough promise at first that in 1835 a large set of six limekilns were built at Bantling Castle near the western foot of Loud Bank incline. In August 1835 it was reported that a man in South Shields 'had known the engines work as late as ten o'clock at night, and as early as three o'clock in the morning'. It was also described that 'the company's engines bring down about 360 loaded wagons daily. The wagons are taken from the depot to the loading-staith as they are wanted. That operation is going on pretty constantly all day'. An engineer of the S&TR, Owen Williams, mentioned how 'the engines do not now run in the night. In the winter the last trains sometimes, but not frequently, ran through the night'. This was backed up by Mr Cresswell, who stated: 'They have now more engines, and can consequently do more work in the day.' By 1835, the S&TR had seven locomotives, six of which were Large Samson 0-4-2 types with a single 2-2-0 Planet-type locomotive.

A prospectus for the Brandling Railway in 1838 mentioned that the Stanhope & Tyne, in 1837, shipped 400,000 tons of coal from South Shields, but of the five riverside coal drops then in use (an increase of the three open in 1835, and later increased to eight) 'all were inadequate to the demand'. It was said that owing to this the Stanhope & Tyne 'for almost half a mile was blackened with wagons ready to be shipped'. More locomotives were purchased, and by 1840 there were eleven locomotives owned and operated by the S&TR, including one, *Projector*, built by the S&TR themselves at South Shields. The expanded locomotive fleet suggests the line had an increasing amount of traffic, but it was also likely linked to the opening of the Durham Junction Railway in 1838 which Thomas Elliot Harrison was also engineer for, and had an arrangement whereby the S&TR provided locomotive power. The S&TR joined the Durham Junction Railway, which ran from Rainton Meadows, near Durham, at a point later known as Washington South Junction. An increase of traffic in the Consett and Annfield area meant that in December 1838 a tender was issued for contractors to work the Stanley and Medomsley levels by locomotive. Certainly, at this point there was no indication that the S&TR was struggling for traffic as the contract was to be for 'a term of years'.

The locomotives employed were described in numerous sources as being *Experiment* built by (Timothy) Hackworth at Shildon, likely the Stockton & Darlington Railway No. 6 *Experiment* (which was originally built by Robert Stephenson & Co. in 1826 as a

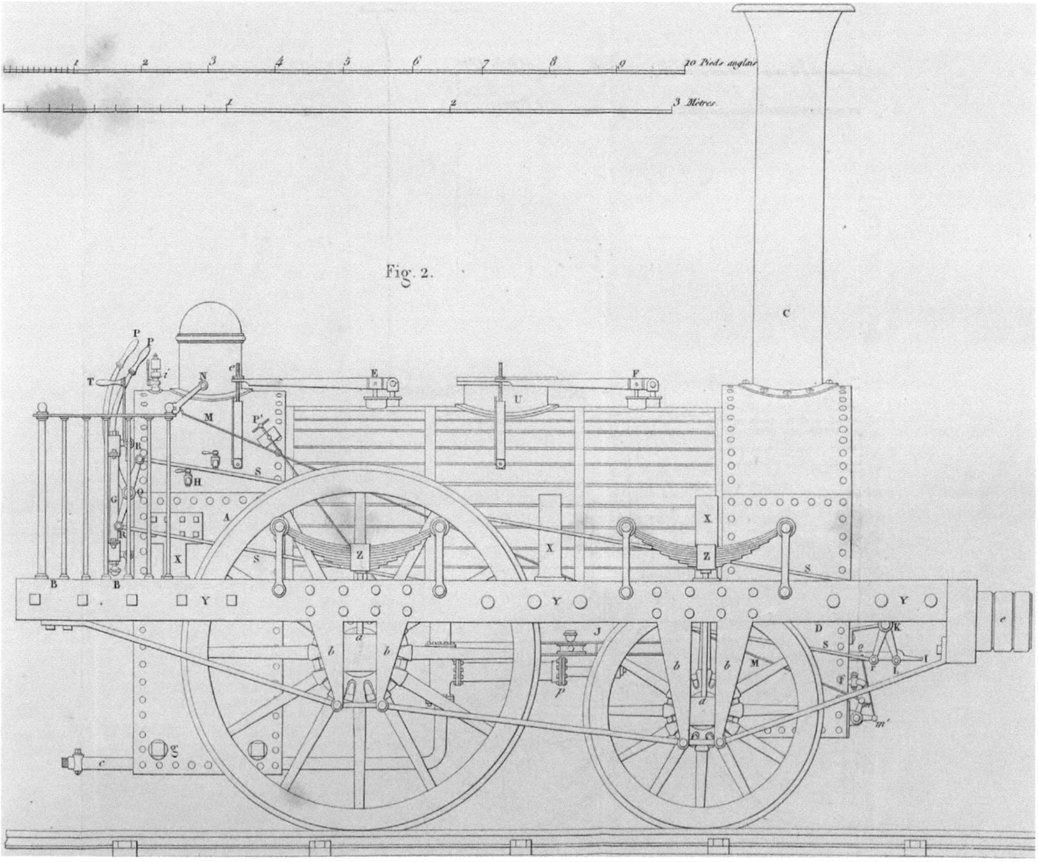

Side profile of a Robert Stephenson & Co. 2-2-0 Planet-type locomotive, as S&TR locomotive *Thomas Newcomen* would have appeared.

four-wheeler and rebuilt by Hackworth as a six-wheeler) and *Blucher* built by (Thomas) Hackworth in Stockton, although no further information is known about this locomotive.

It is likely these locomotives worked one level each. An account published in 1899 of the recollections of William Teasdale mentions the use of locomotives on the Stanley Level. Although both the Stanley and Medomsley levels are described as worked by locomotive in other sources, Teasdale only mentions the Stanley Level, suggesting *Experiment* and *Blucher* both worked it, which could be possible, with a third unknown locomotive working the Medomsley Level. It is also likely his memories, nearly sixty years after the events described, are not fully accurate, as with all personal accounts.

> From Stanley bank head to Annfield Plain, horses were originally employed, but it was found that they were unequal to the work and a locomotive was ordered from a Stockton engine builder which was christened 'Blucher'. The first locomotives on the line were of quaint and primitive type driven by hand gear. One of the earliest was Timothy Hackworth's 'Experiment' which was built at Shildon and sent in charge of

what, in marine circles to-day, would be known as a 'guarantee engineer' known as 'Big Jack'. When Big Jack's time was up, nobody else could be found who could start the engine satisfactorily and he had to be retained.[11]

Teasdale was a contractor for maintenance on the Stanhope & Tyne between the bank foot of Vigo incline and Stanley Bank Head. Teasdale's description mentions that the Pelton Level, originally worked by horses, was afterwards worked by a stationary engine and endless rope. How long this was done for is unknown, but locomotives were working it by the 1850s when an engine shed was built.

The permanent way contractors were paid at a certain rate per mile. They were not just responsible for maintaining the permanent way, but also for clearing all snow falls 'not exceeding three inches in depth' and had to assist the Stanhope & Tyne in clearing heavier falls, along with assisting in the running of the line too. The Stanhope & Tyne directly employed its engine drivers as well as the bankriders, who rode the wagon sets on the inclines, and the brakesmen, who controlled the speed of them, but if they did not turn up for work then the contractor had to cover for them. The bankriders themselves were described as wearing self-made straw hats – the straw plaits and hats were made in downtime while waiting for sets of wagons to be made up for running along the inclines. They were painted in the winter, no doubt in the black tar substance that wagons were painted in to preserve them – similar to what sailors did with their straw hats. Platelayers 'almost invariably' wore tall hats.

On one occasion during the Stanhope & Tyne's working, a bankrider at the foot of an incline gave the signal to start (described as having 'pulled the token') before he attached

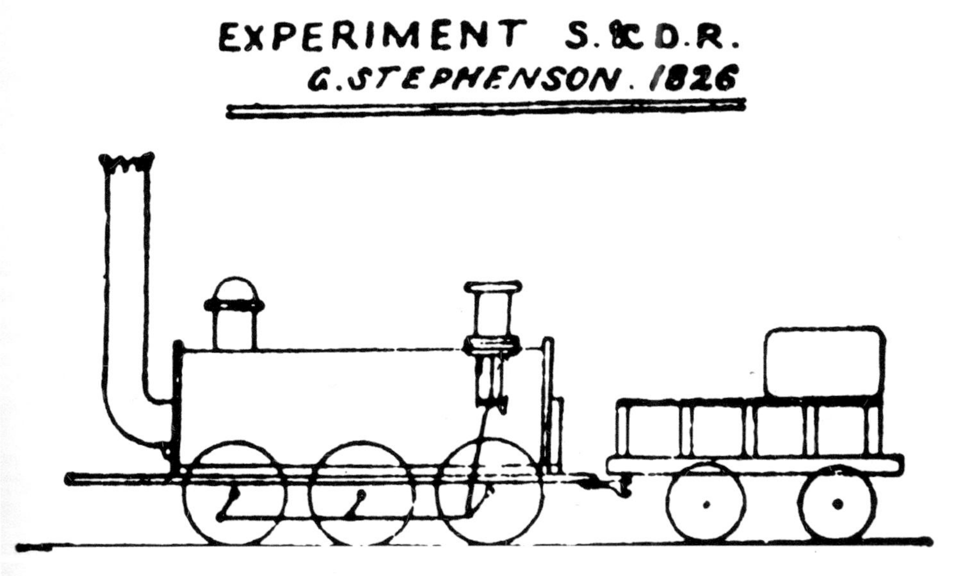

Simple drawing of *Experiment* as rebuilt by Timothy Hackworth and how it would have appeared when it worked on the upper levels of the S&TR in the Stanley and/or Leadgate area. (Theodore West)

The S&TR crossing the road at Annfield Plain, with the Stanhope & Tyne Hotel just visible to the right. (Beamish Museum)

the rope to his set of empty wagons. The loaded set at the top of the incline, having received the signal, was started on its descent without the empty set coupled on to act as a counterweight. It was immediately realised that the brake wheel at the incline head would not be enough to stop a set of loaded wagons, so William Teasdale and others, who were riding the loaded set, applied all the brakes down hard and were able to stop the wagons just after passing the incline foot. The incline was described as 'wrecked' by the action of the thick rope, which should have been attached to the empty set of wagons but instead was being pulled uphill rapidly, lashing around. This was possibly the accident on the Twizell incline reported to T. E. Harrison, engineer of the Stanhope & Tyne, by Joseph Lucas on 25 October 1839, which mentioned an animal potentially being to blame by getting its leg entangled in the signal wire and raising the post. The report mentioned that on the day the report was written, the signal was pulled up twice by a cow getting its leg caught on the signal wire on the Eden Hill incline.

Two flat wagons for lead traffic, known as 'lead bogies', were used for an unusual 'Directors Special' with William Teasdale acting as conductor. The two bogies were arranged to have a fast run along the line, going down Stanley incline by their own momentum after having been brought from Annfield Plain to the bank head by horses. Teasdale had arranged for other horses to be stationed at the bottom of the incline in case they needed a bit more assistance, but Teasdale need not have worried, as after starting

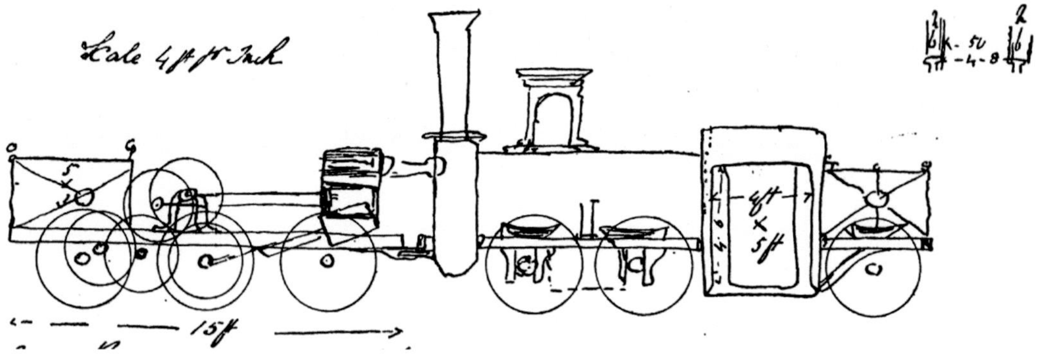

T. E. Harrison was known for his 'patent locomotives' with the boiler on one carriage and working parts, including driving wheels, on another. Two were built for the Great Western Railway, and it is possible that a third was built, as this drawing from Harrison's notebook shows, for the S&TR.

at Stanley bank head the two bogies went all the way to Waldridge bank head without needing any assistance, and only stopped at Waldridge as Robert Stephenson wished to talk to local colliery owners. As time went on, the other directors became impatient and A. J. F. Marreco told Teasdale to proceed, Stephenson having a 'long stern chase' before overtaking the train!

Although there was no passenger service over the Pontop inclines, this did not deter people from riding on wagons, and apparently it was 'no uncommon thing to see even women riding on the coal trucks up and down the inclines on the part of the line over which there was no passenger service'. An event of freak weather known as 'Windy Monday', 7 January 1839, completely stopped all traffic on the line. Some of the Stanhope & Tyne men used a wagon to descend Stanley incline in the belief that the brakes would be able to stop it at the incline foot. The wind was so strong that the wagon kept going at speed down the other inclines and along the level to Waldridge bank head, at which point the men jumped off and the wagon went over the runaway point and was thrown upside-down into an adjacent field. Another curious effect of 'Windy Monday' was that it took the roofs off a lot of miners' houses in the area, and as miners tended to keep pigs in their gardens, many of the now bare rafters were 'adorned by substantial hams and flitches of bacon which waved to and fro in the gale'.

There was an official passenger service on the line between South Shields and the Great North Road near Birtley, running to the Wheatsheaf Inn which still stands. The service was run by one man, with passengers from South Shields walking through the Bridge Inn to get to their train, with the S&TR having a 'coach office' at No. 31 East King Street. The coach was said by William Teasdale to look like a 'typical goods wagon' in 1899, with low sides and a door on each side and benches for seating. Teasdale specifically mentions the carriage 'was drawn by a small four-wheeled locomotive known as "Tommy Newcomen"' (the single 2-2-0 Planet-type locomotive in the S&TR's fleet) from South Shields to Fatfield. From there, onward passengers changed into a similar but smaller carriage for haulage up the Vigo incline (by the stationary engine if there were wagons to go too, if not a horse would take them up the bank) then down the other side to the Great North Road.

Traffic along the S&TR would have been reduced when the Tanfield Moor colliery was won over by the Brandling Railway in November 1840, who had re-laid the 1720s Tanfield Waggonway with iron rails (although the reopening was not ready for some time after the Brandling had said it would be, which meant Tanfield Moor pit was not best pleased). A year earlier, in 1839, the S&TR closed the line from Stanhope to Carr House owing to the disappointingly low levels of sale of lime, and with little other traffic travelling this part of the line, it was shut to reduce costs. It would not be enough to save the S&TR from its debts, and in 1841, it was dissolved.

A typical 1830s open carriage, which matches the description of that used on early passenger services on the line.

The only known photograph of an inclined plane engine house on the P&SSR route – Annfield engine house with its chimney and covered shed for the winding drums visible at the top of Loud Bank, seen in the background of an image of Annfield Plain station being built in the 1890s. (Kind courtesy of Malcolm Charlton, not to be reused)

CHAPTER 2

The Pontop & South Shields Railway

Header image of a P&SSR waybill advertising 'Rates of Charges on Coals & Merchandize'. The image is likely a standard printmakers image of a locomotive, as it shows a 2-2-2 Patentee-type locomotive better suited for fast passenger traffic, although the S&TR and P&SSR used similar 0-4-2 and 0-6-0 locomotives.

The Extraordinary General Meeting of the S&TR held on 29 December 1840 proposed to dissolve the Stanhope & Tyne Railroad Company and form a new one to carry on the railway by shareholders of the S&TR who wished to continue. Those who did not could simply choose not to continue, and although they would lose their shares, they would also lose their responsibilities for the high financial liabilities that the new company had taken on from the S&TR. This was adopted on 2 January 1841, with the S&TR formally dissolved on 5 February 1841. Twenty-five of the original forty-nine S&TR shareholders continued with the Pontop & South Shields Railway, the name showing their interest lay with the eastern half of the railway and they had no interest in the western half; however, despite closing in 1839, owing to the use of wayleaves to build and run the railway, they were still paying for renting the ground. In 1842, this half of the railway was sold to the Derwent Iron Company, who needed it to move limestone from Crawleyside to their new ironworks at Consett – for more information see *The Wear & Derwent Railway* (Fonthill Media, 2022).

A view down the Eden Hill inclined plane. (Beamish Museum)

For the continued operation of the remaining 24½ miles of railway, an Act of Parliament was needed to sanction the selling of the western half and for other arrangements to be made to ensure the railway was not burdened by the same arrangements the S&TR had. The Act was approved on 23 May 1842, with Robert Stephenson elected as chairman. The line continued as it had under S&TR days, but the joining of the railway with the Durham Junction Railway in 1838 was the first of many new railways in the area. Shortly after, the Brandling Railway opened. This crossed the S&TR on the level at Brockley Whins where the railway ran between Gateshead and Sunderland, and at Boldon Lane, where the Brandling Railway, branching from the Sunderland line at Brockley Whins, ran broadly parallel to the S&TR towards South Shields where they had their own passenger station and riverside coal drops on the Tyne. In 1844, the Pontop & South Shields Railway (P&SSR) became part of a much longer route. The Newcastle & Darlington Junction Railway were sanctioned in May to buy the Durham Junction Railway, which they had physically joined by rail a month prior. The P&SSR received authorisation to build a third line of rails between Washington and Boldon for traffic coming north from the Newcastle & Darlington Railway, and built a branch from Boldon to Brockley Whins, involving a timber viaduct over the River Don on the curve between the P&SSR and the Brandling Railway. As a result of this, on 24 May 1844, a special train pulled by the *Cleveland* locomotive of the Newcastle & Darlington Junction Railway was able to run from York, from the Durham Junction Railway, then along the P&SSR between Washington and Brockley Whins, then onto the Brandling to Gateshead. A longer route was possible via numerous other railways, and on 18 June 1844 the line was opened with a special train run from Euston Square, London, to Gateshead, running at an average speed of 37 mph and being in motion for eight hours and eleven minutes. A dinner provided by the Newcastle & Darlington Junction Railway that evening in Newcastle included George Stephenson himself describing his building of his first steam locomotive at Killingworth some thirty years before. Passenger services to the public began on 19 June, worked by locomotives of the Great North of England Railway, taking twelve and a half hours between London and Gateshead (two and three-quarter hours of which were stoppages i.e. watering, coaling). The 247-foot-long wooden trestle viaduct between the P&SSR and Brandling over the River Don lasted until it was demolished owing to decay and little use at the end of 1940, its condition worsened by a fire in 1939.[1] The use of the P&SSR for the East Coast Mainline route lasted until 1850, when a new line was opened between Washington and Pelaw.

The initial fleet of the P&SSR was that taken over from the S&TR, consisting of a mixture of 0-4-2s and 0-6-0s of Robert Stephenson's Large Samson design, and the single 2-2-0 Planet-type engine. As of 31 December 1844, there were thirteen locomotives in the P&SSR fleet. The running of multiple railways linked together, and with trains running over several different railway company's metals, was an administrative nightmare, and

North Eastern Railway B Class (later N8 Class) 0-6-2T No. 1124 working the Pelton Level and seen at the head of Waldridge incline. It is looking away from the incline and sat in the central road which was used for loaded coal wagons to go down the incline – the empty sets would arrive on one of the raised 'kips' on either side of the lower central road. A loaded set is visible behind on the central road, and lamps over the railway enable working at night. (Beamish Museum)

George Hudson, the 'Railway King' and chairman of the Newcastle & Darlington Railway, looked to bring them together. The P&SSR was taken over in 1845 by the Newcastle & Darlington Railway, joining the Brandling and Durham Junction railways who had joined in 1844. Although taken over by the Newcastle & Darlington Railway, the P&SSR remained independent until two years later when the Newcastle & Darlington Railway, and therefore the P&SSR, became part of the York, Newcastle & Berwick Railway on the first day of 1847. The end of the P&SSR's existence saw it sell its collieries, originally owned by the S&TR, and the P&SSR line joined George Hudson's empire. George Hudson, who had the foresight to bring together many of Britain's scattered railway companies to create wider networks, using an inherited fortune and aided by being able to persuade investors to back him and the companies, was brought down – although never actually prosecuted – by alleged improper accounting practices in 1849, which those who disliked him were all too keen to take advantage of. This has left a mark on his name, but it cannot be denied that he left an incredible legacy in Britain's railway network, especially in the North East.[2]

In terms of the operating of the railway itself, nothing would have drastically changed in its appearance and operation as the owning companies changed. The original P&SSR locomotives were renumbered 82–94 in the York, Newcastle & Berwick Railway fleet. Following the construction of *Projector* at South Shields by the S&TR in 1839, locomotives continued to be built at South Shields, with four 2-4-0 York, Newcastle & Berwick locomotives built here, numbering 95, 96, 98 and 99. Coal continued to be moved as the pits expanded their operations and new ones opened, and some form of passenger service appears to have continued running on the line. In 1848, a group of men who had been repairing the Vigo engine were returning to South Shields in a second-class carriage hauled by an engine driven by a man named Lawson. After leaving Vigo the train travelled slowly to Washington station where one man got off, then continued at a speed of about 14 mph to the Don watering place, stopping to take on water. As the engine started to be watered,

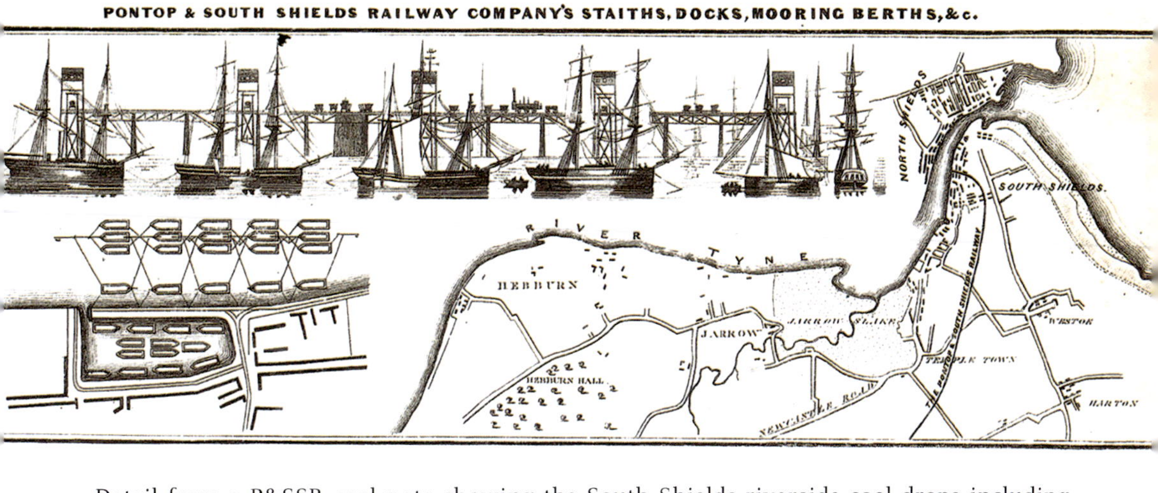

Detail from a P&SSR coal note showing the South Shields riverside coal drops including a locomotive and chaldrons, route of the railway through South Shields, and the planned Tyne Dock, which was over a decade away. (Kind courtesy of Christopher Dean, not to be reused)

Lawson started to oil the locomotive when the mail train crashed into the stationary train. Of the seventeen men in the carriage, several jumped out before the collision but three were killed and another badly injured. The fireman had jumped into a hedge and Lawson had just got the train moving, presumably to mitigate the effects of the crash. Lawson suffered a broken arm but was able to stop the engine near Boldon. The two crew of the mail train were also injured. The cause was thought due to Lawson not having a watch (although company rules were that all engine drivers were to have watches) and presumably thought the mail train had already passed, but did not ask at any of the crossing gates where he could have asked the gatekeepers.[3]

Eden Colliery, built alongside the P&SSR in 1844 near Leadgate. The opening and expanding of pits near the P&SSR ensured this line became increasingly busy. In the distance, the railway can be seen continuing over a bridge near the Jolly Drovers pub and into Leadgate. (Beamish Museum)

CHAPTER 3

The North Eastern Railway

Major changes would come to the P&SSR line following the formation, in 1854, of the North Eastern Railway (NER). The York, Newcastle & Berwick Railway joined the York & North Midland Railway, the Leeds Northern Railway and the Malton & Driffield Railway to form this new railway. The NER would continue to acquire other railways in its area (including the Stockton & Darlington Railway in the 1860s, although that line continued to have an independent existence within the NER for over a decade more) and came to have a near-monopoly on public railways in the North East. Key behind its strength was the money to be made in the movement of coal.

A set of empty hoppers arriving at the head of Stanley incline on the raised 'kip'. The bankrider is on a P5 10-ton hopper holding onto the brake handle and is about to kick the quoit to open the lock chain and disconnect the set from the incline rope. (*The Railway Magazine*)

As Revd Wrenford of the parish of Jarrow was on his way to church on Sunday 16 September 1855, he heard the noise of workmen on the Pontop branch. With this being an unlawful offence Revd Wrenford informed the police, who then visited the line and took the names of the three men who appeared to be overseeing the work repairing the line – William Jackson, Forster Lishman and George Storey. The men were summoned to South Shields Police Court 'for unlawfully working on Sunday'. The following Wednesday, the men's solicitor, Mr Hodge, objected that it seemed only men in the NER's employ were singled out for prosecution as there had been none similar until two NER employees were fined in October 1854, and 'there could be no doubt that in the borough there was Sunday trading by others'. One of the Joicey family, who owned coal mines in the area, spoke in defence that 'the railway company were compelled to do those particular repairs on a Sunday, and there unless they did so, from 8,000 to 10,000 must of necessity be laid off work'. Despite this, the magistrates 'considered the case proved' and fined each of the three men 5*s* and costs.[1]

The P&SSR line, which was built for and remained extremely busy on account of its movement of coal, was soon identified by the NER for needing improvement, both in terms of the line itself and the shipping facilities on the Tyne. Shipping coal via the Tyne was hampered by the limited shipping facilities of the former Stanhope & Tyne and Brandling Junction Railways, with Sunderland having greater facilities for shipment; however, this increased the journey the coal needed to be taken, and therefore the expense.

Interior of the brake cabin at Eden Hill. (Beamish Museum)

To allow for locomotive working from South Shields all the way up to the foot of the Waldridge incline, work was undertaken to allow the Vigo engine to be taken out of service. It is not known if the High Flatts engine was still in use at this point, or whether the development of more powerful locomotives meant it was simply removed – the 1857 surveyed map shows a potential inclined plane engine house by the line near South Pelaw colliery. A notice to contractors was issued by NER Secretary W. O'Brien on 18 April 1856 for tenders to be received 'for the execution of the EARTH-WORK, MASONRY and LAYING of the PERMANENT WAY, in altering the line from Fatfield to Stella Gill, upon their Pontop Branch Railway, in length about 3¼ miles'.[2] On 13 June an agreement was made with Lord Durham to purchase additional land to allow the work at Vigo to take place.

The work also saw the replacement of the level crossing over the Great North Road at Birtley with a wooden overbridge in 1857 (the still standing iron bridge replaced it in 1893) and following the completion locomotives worked the line from Stella Gill to South Shields. As part of this work, an existing junction with the Beamish Waggonway (which now shipped its coals via the P&SSR, after originally having wharves for keels on the banks of the River Wear) was moved to the west side of the Great North Road. A four-road engine shed was built at Stella Gill, authorised in 1857, capable of housing two 0-6-0s on each track and with eight cottages for workers. The shed also had a 50-foot turntable and was later closed in the 1890s, likely as a result of the later line avoiding the inclines.[3]

The Annfield Plain area had two engine sheds in place by the 1850s: the town itself, where a two-road shed existed for working between Annfield Plain and Stanley bank head,

A poor-quality but rare view of an NER 0-6-2T crossing the line at Annfield Plain on the original route of the line. The Stanhope & Tyne public house was to the right (south-east) side of the crossing. (Beamish Museum)

and a small single road shed on the other side of the inclined planes, at Bantling Castle near the limekilns. It is possible these two engine sheds dated back to the late 1830s when locomotives first worked these levels between inclined planes. Another engine shed was in place in the 1850s on the Pelton Level between the Eden Hill and Waldridge inclines. The workshops at South Shields would have remained as a base for locomotives too, at the other end of the main locomotive-worked section of the line – although this area was later cleared when a new passenger station was built in 1879, by which point locomotives working the line would have been based at Tyne Dock.

The NER's directors' report to shareholders at the half-yearly meeting in August 1858 stated that the 'alterations on the Pontop Branch have been completed, and the advantages which were expected to be derived from them are being fully realised'.[4] Some idea of the scale of the works can be gathered by the list of items that were advertised as to be sold by auction in January 1859 by Messrs Forster and Lawton following completion of their contracts on the Pontop branch. Heading the list was a six-wheeled locomotive engine 'with four wheels 4½ ft diameter, being coupled, Copper Fire-Box, Brass Tubes, 14-inch Cylinder, 18-inch Stroke, and Four-wheeled TENDER' (which could be one of the Stanhope & Tyne's original 0-4-2s, or at least very similar), ten side and end tipping contractors' earth wagons, together with 'numerous' stone trucks, stone bogies, dobbin carts, various types of cranes and winches, 'patent piling and machinery', a 'pipe and tile machine', 60 tons of contractors' malleable iron rails together with malleable wagon axles and wheels, and a variety of bolts, screws, spikes, clips, anvils, wooden blocks, sling chains, wire ropes, and around eighty wheelbarrows. Amongst various quantities and types of wood there were sixty 'Seasoned New Panel-Doors, Sash Windows, &c' which together with 'numerous House-Stoves' indicates disassembled temporary workers' accommodation for the navvies who undertook the work.[5]

A new pumping engine that provided water to locomotives near Stella Gill was built in 1858 and caused injury to a man superintending it in April. A man named Storey, who was foreman 'at the standing engine on the Pontop and Stanhope Railway', was stood with his right foot close to a crank connected to the flywheel of the engine, the crank moving through a hole in the floor. Storey was clearly stood too close as the crank hit his foot, with the result that 'three of his toes were instantly cut off'. He was then taken home where a week later was said to be 'progressing favourably'.[6]

Fireman William Gilroy was uncoupling wagons at Stella Gill in December 1858, and when the locomotive moved, what is described as a 'horse crook' of a coal wagon (likely meaning the long brake lever) caught Gilroy's jacket, throwing him to the ground and a rake of about fifteen empty wagons went over him. He was taken home to Cambridge Street, South Shields, but died about three hours after, from his injuries.[7] In March 1859, another fatality occurred on the line, this time at Boldon station. Mineral train guard William Sotheron was uncoupling coal wagons – likely for the coal depot now at Beamish Museum – when he was accidentally crushed to death.[8]

Facilities for shipping coal from the Tyne were greatly improved in 1859 with the opening of Tyne Dock, 4 miles from the mouth of the Tyne near Jarrow and South Shields. When it fully opened in March, Tyne Dock had a colossal basin of 50 acres, with four jetties running into the dock, two specifically for loading coal with the other two for ballast and goods. The creation of a large dock with a focus on shipping coal had been proposed in the

The top deck of one of the four Tyne Dock coal staiths. The rails were arranged so that a loaded wagon would run down to the spout, and then back when empty, by gravity, clearly seen here in the 1930s. (Kind courtesy of Malcolm Charlton, not to be reused)

1830s with a company set up, but the sheer expense involved meant it was not until the creation of the North Eastern Railway and its financial clout that it became a possibility.

In 1860 it shipped nearly 1½ million tons of coal and coke, and double that ten years later. By 1911, Tyne Dock had sixteen berths for emptying coal into the waiting ships along four huge jetties projecting into the dock, which formed distinctive arches over the dockside road. By the time Tyne Dock was under construction, technology was changing the shipping too, with wooden colliers being replaced by larger iron-built vessels powered by steam.

On the night of 23 September 1861, locomotive No. 84 was stood at Stella Gill attached to a train of loaded coal wagons ready for Tyne Dock. There were three crew – driver John Smith, fireman William Hunter, and guard John Leatham – who had been stood on the tender talking to the others. Leatham went to the front end of the locomotive, and it was described that he 'had scarcely got there when the engine exploded with awful violence, rending itself to pieces, and scattering fragments of the boiler and machinery in every direction. Several persons standing about had narrow escapes.' Leatham was killed instantly, with Smith and Hunter both severely injured and taken swiftly to South Shields. Hunter was described as unconscious the next day.[9] The engine was 'shattered to pieces by the explosion'.[10] The engine had been repaired two years and five months previously,

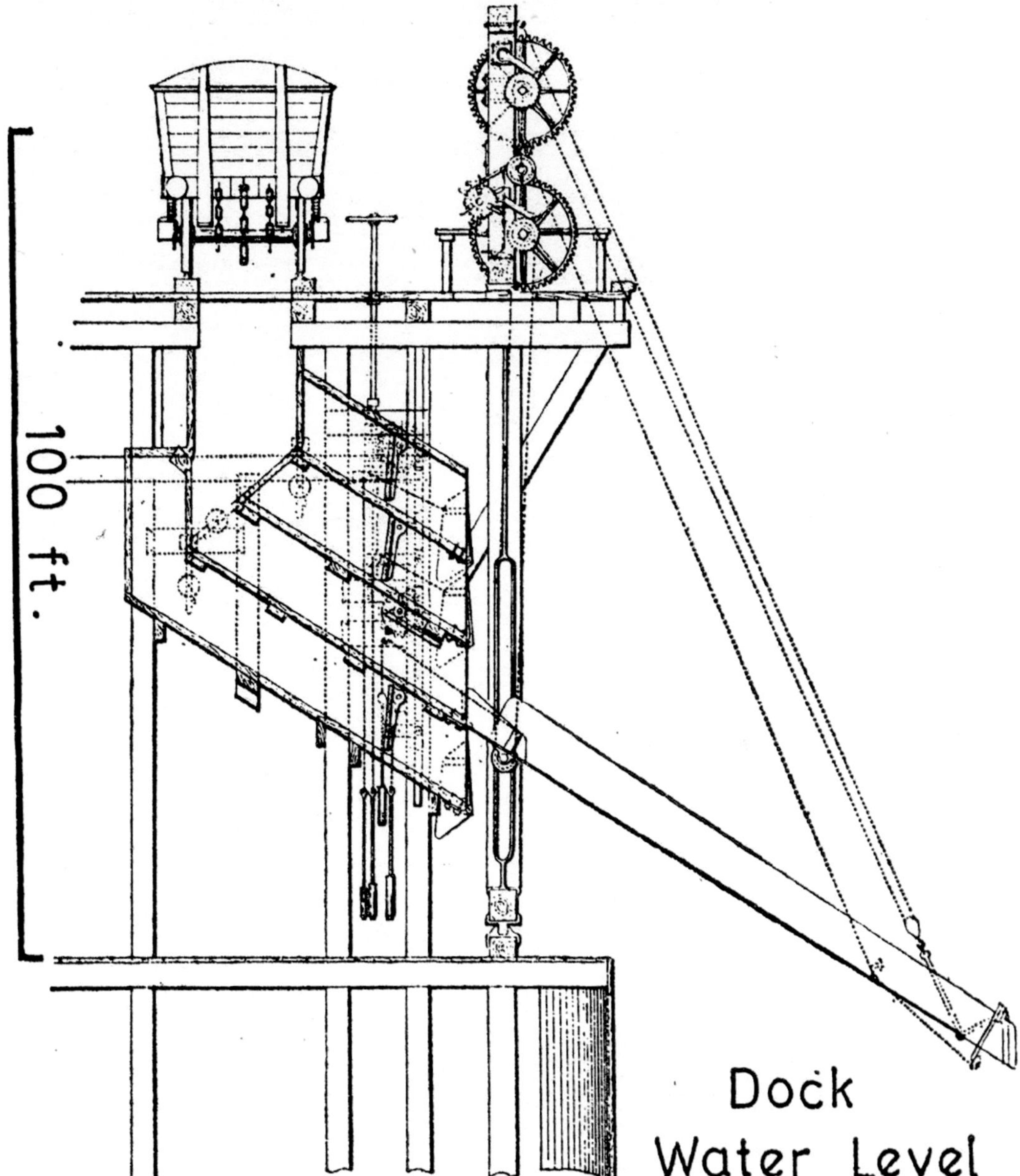

A diagram showing the method of unloading coal hoppers onto ships at Tyne Dock when it first opened.

but the boiler plates were not looked at. It was considered that the weakness in the plates would have been noticed if they had been tested more recently.[11]

The locomotive, No. 84, was built in 1853 by the York, Newcastle & Berwick Railway shortly before it became the NER and had been in service since December of that year. It was an 0-6-0 with a working pressure of 100psi, which it was at when the explosion

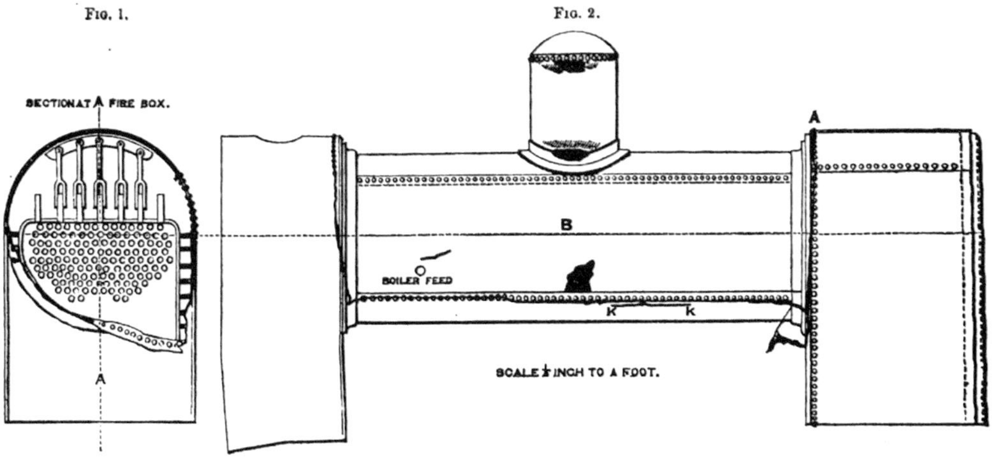

Detail from the Board of Trade report showing the damage done to the boiler of locomotive No. 84 after its explosion at Stella Gill.

occurred. The explosion tore the boiler barrel, which was 10 feet long and 3½ feet wide, and made of four 10-foot-long plates joined by longitudinal lap seams, 'open from end to end, along a seam of rivets on the left side, about 14 inches from the bottom; to bend it over to the right across the other line of rails, and to throw off the dome, partly by striking it against some other object, and partly from the effect of its own momentum, as it was wrung round with great violence'. The force of the explosion appears to have lifted the engine off the rails, landing close by. The remains of the locomotive clearly showed that corrosion had occurred for a length of 21 inches along the boiler plate which burst, the metal thinning so much 'that the force of steam was too great for it to resist; and when once the steam and water found an opening through it, the remainder was torn, and the sounder portions of the plate gave way, as always happens under such circumstances, with comparatively little difficulty'.[12] The investigation recommended more inspections and examinations should be made of boilers, and also criticised how the firebox end of the boiler was fixed securely to the locomotive's frame by hanging brackets rather than one end (usually the firebox end) fixed to the frames by sliding angle iron so as the boiler heated up and cooled it would not cause strain between the boiler and frame as the boiler expanded and contracted.[13]

An eleven-year-old boy, Thomas Punshon, engaged as a messenger between Stella Gill and Waldridge, was killed as he headed home from Waldridge to Edmondsley on the evening of 20 February 1865. It appears he was walking on the Waldridge incline when a set of wagons soon overtook him. Punshon tried to jump on the first wagon but missed his hold and fell onto the rails, with twelve wagons running him over and killing him instantly. He had been previously warned repeatedly about getting on the wagons, but sadly was to pay for taking no heed of this with his life.

A local girl, Eilen Ratcliffe, aged just ten years old, was brought up on a warrant in front of Revd H. Barrett in August 1868 following serious incidents on the Pontop inclines. There had been numerous incidents of pieces of wood placed on the rails, including an occasion

Brake cabin at Waldridge bank head. Note the signalling apparatus which was wound at either end to indicate sets of wagons ready to travel along the incline. (Beamish Museum)

These 4-ton 'Black Waggons' were still in use at Seaham Harbour until the 1960s, allowing them to be saved by Beamish Museum. They are nearly identical to the NER's P1 4-ton 'Black Waggons'.

when a bankrider 'had to jump off at the imminent risk of his life to remove another piece from the rails'. A watch was kept on the line the day after and the girl was seen going on it near No Place, looking around, then putting a piece of wood on the line. The watcher spoke to her and 'she did not deny the offence'. With such a serious risk to life it was mentioned that, by law, the girl should be taken to trial at the next assizes and would be at risk of penal transportation to Australia (a practice that ceased later that year). After deliberation, sentence was reserved with her father 'entering into recognizances of £20 to bring her up for judgment when called upon to do so'. The girl was remarked as being in tears during the whole session and 'evidently had no idea of such a termination to her actions'.[14]

In the 1870s coal was still being carried in chaldron-type wagons, not dissimilar from those used since the opening of the railway in the 1830s. Their capacity had been increased with a larger design to 4 tons, and they were known as Black Waggons to distinguish them from the slightly smaller chaldrons, although the name 'chaldron' remained to refer to them, including to the NER whose P1 Black Waggon-type hoppers were described as chaldrons in official literature. At this time, the Waldridge incline moved about eighty full sets of these wagons a day, carrying about 64 tons of coal each (about sixteen wagons per set), with the Stanley and Eden Hill inclines carrying about ⅔ of this. Shunting engines referred to as 'pilots' at either side of the Waldridge incline were uncommon, with a horse stationed at Waldridge Bank Foot in the 1870s in case of incorrect shunting to rectify errors before a larger locomotive came to take the sets of wagons away. Sprags (a short but thick wooden stick or bar) were used to stop the wagons and for shunting, and 'all the men on the inclines were experts at this class of work'. On 14 March 1870, on the first of what was to be fifty-five years of railway service by J. Hutton, at the time a sheave oiler on the Eden Hill and Stanley inclines, a set of goods wagons were heading up the Waldridge incline with a load of flour and other goods for the Craghead Co-operative Society. The bankrider noticed that the points at the 'meetings' halfway along the incline (where the wagon sets would pass) were set incorrectly, meaning the loaded coal wagons coming downhill would collide into the uphill goods. To prevent this, the bankrider detached the rope from the coupling, meaning his set of wagons immediately started to runaway downhill, preventing the otherwise inevitable collision. Releasing the set, as counterweight to the loaded set coming downhill, did mean that the loaded coal wagons picked up speed too and followed down the incline at speed, meeting the goods wagons near the foot of Waldridge incline. The collision sent broken wagons, coal, flour and other groceries scattering around the area. Broken wagons were on the roof of the railwaymen's messroom at Waldridge Bank Foot, and a wagon of flour was emptied into the pantry of a railway worker's cottage nearby, although the occupant's 'only regret was that the pantry was not large enough to hold the "gift"'. Despite the mess, there was no injury to anyone involved.

The level crossing on Eden Hill incline. (*The Railway Magazine*)

An odd case occurred on the morning of 28 November 1874 on the P&SSR. As an engine pulling a train of empty coal wagons was passing Pontop weigh house at a speed of around 20 mph in order to go up the Pontop incline, nineteen-year-old spragger Richard Cresswell threw a sprag at the engine, causing it to jump heavily and come to a standstill, the sprag being found between the middle wheel and horn plate. The only reason for this action, mentioned at the trial, was presented by the defence, Mr Wright, who suggested that Cresswell may have stopped the train in order that he could get on it and ride it to his destination. He was found guilty by the jury, but they recommended mercy and Cresswell was sentenced to one week imprisonment, having already been imprisoned previously.[15] An incident involving cows took place on 29 August 1876 as two sets of wagons were about to pass each other on the Stanley incline, one of the sets (presumably the set going uphill) running into some cows which had got onto the railway. This threw the wagons off the rails, jerking the wire rope and breaking it, meaning the other set ran down the incline and crashed into the other set, killing an old woman who was riding on the buffers of one of the sets of wagons. The newspaper report described her as being 'found cut to pieces'. Additionally, three of the cows were killed.

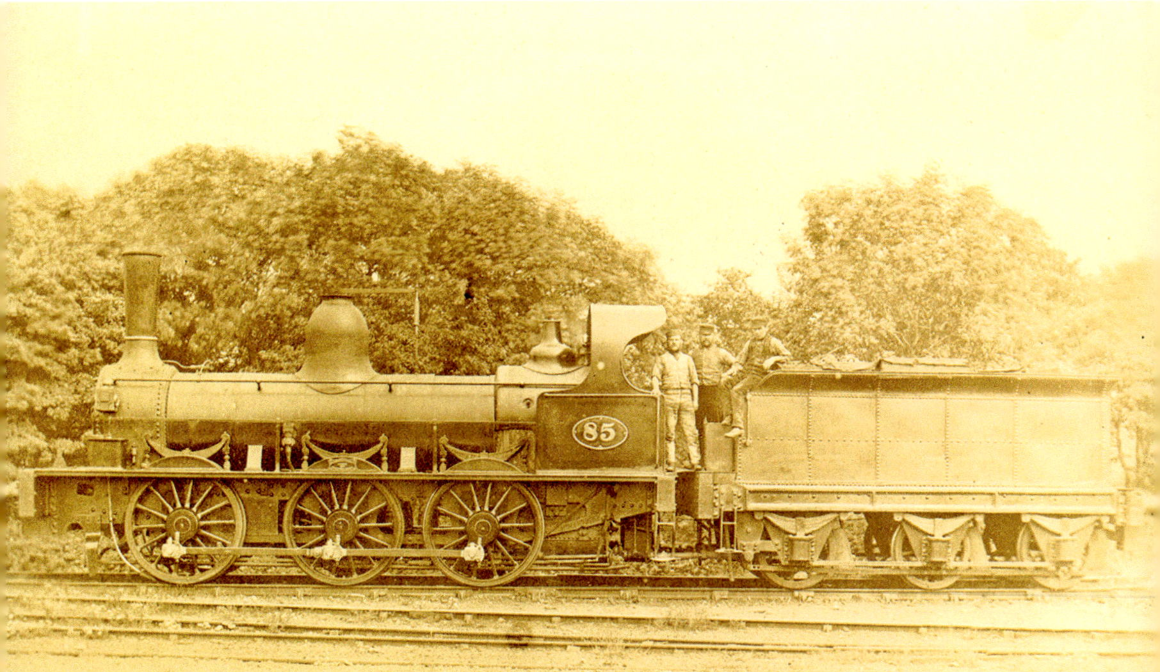

Locomotive No. 85 at Stella Gill on 5 August 1878. Fireman Ralph Charlton stood on the left. He started on the NER in 1872 as a guard, becoming a fireman in 1873 and then being promoted to driver at Tyne Dock on 10 January 1888. (Kind courtesy of Malcolm Charlton, not to be reused)

CHAPTER 4

Avoiding the Inclines

The continuing increase of mineral traffic on the line, and output from the ironworks at Consett, meant a line avoiding the inclined planes was needed. The first move was to avoid the inclines at Annfield Plain. The first deviation around Loud Hill and its inclines was planned in 1875, but did not happen, and in 1882 a longer route had its Act of Parliament passed. This 2-mile-long deviation swept to the south of Loud Hill, leaving the original 1834 route to the east of Loud Hill before the S&TR crossed the road through Annfield Plain, and on its new route crossing over the road to Stanley by a bridge and continuing to run to the south of Annfield Plain and Greencroft, joining the original route again at East Castle, near the now-disused S&TR Bantling Castle limekilns. Although the inclined planes were taken out of service, on the west side of the deviation the original route was partly used for sidings, and on the eastern side the line continued over the road to the engine sheds, and to serve pits, this section continuing in use for decades to come. The new deviation opened on 1 January 1886, allowing locomotives to work from Consett to the head of Stanley incline.

Whilst this work was taking place, local coal owners, who were aggrieved at the NER's high prices for moving coal, raised a new scheme to build a line from Pelton to Dunston where coal would be shipped, separate from the NER. Owing to the swing bridge opening on the Tyne in 1876, it was now possible for ships to sail further upstream on the Tyne for loading with coal. This scheme, the West Durham & Tyne Railway, had its bill fail at Parliament owing to the NER's case for its existing railway and facilities in the area, and what it planned to do in the future. What this scheme did achieve though, was to shock the NER into making further improvements in the area.

Avoiding the three Pontop inclines was the next improvement on the line, something which would clearly involve substantial earthworks and excavations, and severe gradients to climb from Stella Gill to Annfield Plain. The Act of Parliament for this passed in May 1887, the route leaving the 1834 line at South Pelaw junction which was half a mile east of Stella Gill, and ran to the north of the 1834 route, never more than a mile away (geographically, not by rail) from the original line, and going via Pelton, Beamish and Shield Row, joining the 1834 route only shortly before the beginning of the 1886 deviation just to the east of Annfield Plain. The work on the deviation began in 1890. To maintain a gradual climb up to Annfield Plain, many embankments and cuttings were required,

Q6 Class locomotive passing through the Greencroft cutting on the 1886 deviation. (Beamish Museum)

with the most impressive being the mile-long cutting at Beamish which also had two short tunnels under the Beamish Waggonway. This cutting alone saw around quarter of a million cubic yards of soil removed, passing through Hell Hole Wood. The deviation, and its allowing locomotive working along the route from the East Coast Mainline to Consett and beyond, meant passenger services could finally be introduced. Stations were built at Pelton, Beamish, Shield Row and Annfield Plain, the line from Annfield Plain to Consett not being suitable at this time for passenger traffic – it was still single line west of the 1886 deviation at East Castle. The NER discussed the point that wooden structures for the station buildings would be just as expensive as stone, as wood, in time, decayed and needed repair/replacement as well as frequent repainting. Despite this, the stations, warehouses and signal boxes on the line were made of wood, although fears of subsidence owing to the heavy mining in the area could have been the reason for this. Additionally, rather than at the station themselves, housing for the stationmasters and porters were to be located, where possible, close to colliery buildings.

As part of the work, Ouston Junction was built, a curve from the line which joined it to the East Coast Mainline, which opened on 16 October 1893, followed by the deviation line from South Pelaw to Annfield Plain opening for goods and mineral traffic on 13 November. The passenger service started later, with the first passenger train from Newcastle to Annfield Plain running on 1 February 1894. The train called at Bensham, Low Fell and Birtley on the East Coast Mainline before running on to the P&SSR line to stop at Pelton, Beamish, Shield

Workers during the construction of the 1893 deviation. (Beamish Museum)

Row and ending at Annfield Plain. The day was marked by 'general rejoicings and great excitement' with shops in Annfield Plain and West Stanley closing, with most workmen taking the day as a holiday.[1] It was also heralded in song, written by 'The Pitman Poet' Tommy Armstrong, who lived in the area and wrote about events affecting it, featuring his distinctive North West Durham accent and referencing Shield Row, Annfield Plain, and locations in Newcastle such as the Empire Theatre on Newgate ('Neugit') Street.

Th' Nue Ralewae Te Anfeeld Plane
It wis in the month e November.
En ipon th' thorteenth dae,
Th' eer in hiteen ninety three,
When th' nue ralewae
Wis oapind oot for minoril,
For th' cumpiny wis flade
Te trust th' lives e wor cany aud wives,
Th' line been nuely lade.

Spoken

It wis vary thowtfil e th' ralewae cumpiny te trie th' line we deed stock forst, but thor wid nivor been e ralewae muaid tiv Anfeeld Plane if it hadnit been Billy Bulmore, Ridily, th' owerseeor, en Bil Indyan, West Stanla, en th' oanly wae thit we cin recompense thim is we singen th' chorus-

Q6 Class locomotive on the 1893 deviation between Stanley and Annfield Plain. The photographer took the image from the 1834 S&TR route. (Beamish Museum)

Chorus

We'll sing in praise e Bully Bulmore,
Ridily en Indyan th' suaim,
We shud trie it th' next big elechshin
Te put M.P. te thor nuaim,
If ther awn expense for th'
Cuntry-side
Thae laibor'd neet en dae,
Lang mae th' liv for te ride up en doon
Ipin th' nue ralewae.
Wen hitten ninety fower cum in
The tauk wis neet en dae,
Wunderen wen the tranes wid start
Ipon th' nue raleway.
Genueiry past en went,
En eesed es e wor pane,
Februairy th' forst com in,
En browt es th' mornen trane.

Annfield Plain station.

Spoken
Ye shud see th' cany aud wives gigin eboot, sum
We th' glass e thor hand—hauf tite, drinken e helth te th'
Nue raleway. Tripey Nan shoots: join we me en we'll sing-

Chorus
Mony e scor freh Stanla went,
Likewis freh Tanfeeld Lee,
En met it Sheel Raw staishin,
Th' mornen trane te see.
Wen thare ard th' wussil blaw
It set th' plaice elive,
Three cheers went up freh yung en aud,
Wen th' forst trane did erive.

Spoken
Aw wis stanen beside a chep wen th' shooten started, aul nivor forget it, he vary neer shifted my nolidge box off its plaicem, he had hes mooth wide oapen, it just put e th' mind iv e empty hoose, he had nee teeth in, aw cud see reet doon hes throate en neerly throo th' back door, but aw shifted me stand en began to sing—

Chorus
There wis money a score got in
Te ride the Annfeeld Plane,

Just te sae thaid ad e ride,
In th' forst nue ralewae trane.
Two cany awd fish wives, like the rest
Th' sade thaid geten thor wish,
Thae wid oftin be oot e th' cuntry noo
We thor baskets en thor fish.

Spoken

Jack Smith had a gam cock clocken, en he wis doon it Bob Johnstin's it Sheel Raw, geten e clecken e weel bred eggs, he ad six e one pockit en sivin e the turthor, but wen he got tiv Anfeeld Plane he oanly ad two, the carrigis war that full his eggs wis awl broken, when he gat yem he put he's cote under the clocker, he still expects te git th' breed, aw wish he may, aw left im thare singen—

Chorus

If ye want to gan te th' peopil's paliss,
Or th' Neugit Street Impire,
Ye heh nee caul te bothor yor heed,
E cab or e trap te hire.
Th' tranes is runen for te sute es awl
Ipon th' Sheel Raw line,
Ye can gan e th' mornen or the eftorneun,
For te' see th' pantomime-

Annfield Plain station under construction, apparently after suffering storm damage. (Kind courtesy of Malcolm Charlton, not to be reused)

Pelton station. (Beamish Museum)

The passenger service gap between Annfield Plain and the Consett area was, of course, far from desirable. On the other side of Consett was Blackhill station, which had connections via the Derwent Valley to Newcastle via Rowlands Gill, down to Durham via Lanchester, or, via the S&TR's western half and joining the Stockton & Darlington Railway route, down towards Tow Law, Bishop Auckland and Darlington. The NER was due to ask for tenders to widen the line between East Castle and Consett which would allow double track, when the Consett Iron Company opposed the work. The iron company were of the opinion that introducing a passenger service on this section would 'interfere' with traffic to and from the ironworks. This was not a complaint to be taken lightly. The ironworks was a major provider of traffic for the area, and their introduction of steelmaking in the 1880s had seen a further increase in traffic requiring the NER to build more sidings. In the event, the iron company must have been satisfied with the NER's discussions regarding the issue, as the tenders were issued in the summer, and on 17 August 1896 the first passenger train from Newcastle via Annfield Plain ran to Blackhill, via the new stations at Leadgate and Consett and a new curve onto the Derwent Valley line, which had been built in 1893. Although the service had no formal ceremony, it was still met by large crowds at Leadgate and Consett.[2] Some sixty-two years after the S&TR had opened through the area, the towns along the route in North West Durham now had a passenger service, with five services each way on weekdays.

The locomotive-worked line from the East Coast Mainline to Consett, running over the 1886 and 1893 deviations along with the original S&TR, became known as the Birtley,

Above: An atmospheric photograph of a passenger train leaving Leadgate station en route to Consett, hauled by a McDonnell 59 Class 0-6-0. (Beamish Museum)

Below: Map showing the general location of lines, stations and pits in the area around the 1893 deviation and original S&TR route.

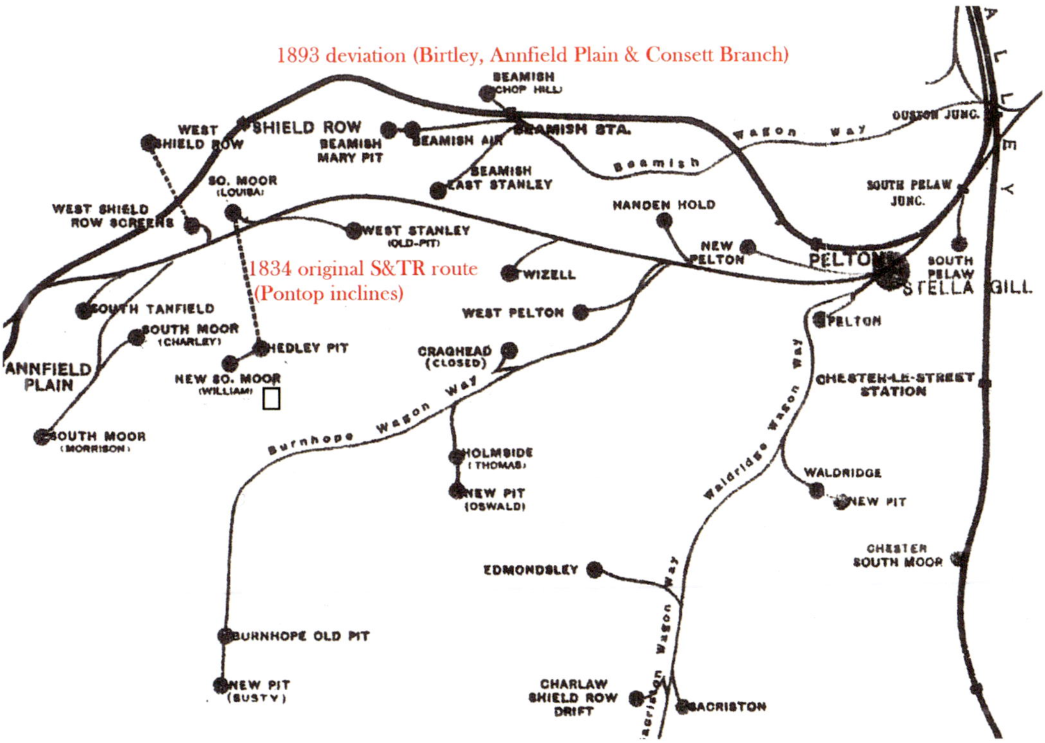

Annfield Plain & Consett branch, or just the Annfield Plain branch. It also became known as the Tyne Dock to Consett line, mirroring the shift of focus away from South Shields following the opening of Tyne Dock and the engine shed there, with the South Shields end of the line becoming home in the late nineteenth century to the new passenger station for that town. The book's focus continues on the line from Tyne Dock to Consett, including the original Pontop inclines route. Improvements elsewhere aided the shipment of coal from the line too. To increase capacity on the Tyne, a set of staiths were built on the south bank of the Tyne at Dunston in 1893. The huge set of wooden staiths, said to be the largest timber structure in Europe, jutted into the river with three berths on each side. A new set of staiths called Dunston West were later built to increase the capacity for shipping coal from here.

In dense fog on the morning of 19 February 1896, just before noon, Long Boiler Class 0-6-0 locomotive No. 1743 pulling nine loaded wagons was at Carr House on its way between Consett and Annfield Plain when it collided into the back of a stationary empty goods train. The locomotive and some portion of the railway was damaged, but the driver and fireman were uninjured as they had remained at their positions until just before the impact, jumping off before so. The guard of the goods train, Thomas Ayre, was thrown from his seat into the middle of the brake van but was otherwise fine.[3]

The monthly meeting of West Stanley Urban District Council in April 1897 raised the issue of Oxhill railway crossing, owing to 'the delay and obstruction caused to both vehicular and passenger traffic'. It was agreed that representation would be made to the NER to 'insist on the removal of the cause of the obstruction'.[4] The level crossing, despite the heavy road traffic backups it caused, was never removed or replaced by a bridge and continued to be a hindrance until the 1970s.

The trains, and the stations they called at, became a part of the social fabric of people's lives, with events taking place involving them reported on over the years giving an understanding of life in general but also the experience of travelling on, or being near, the railway. On the night of 6 October 1896, a little girl's dress caught fire from the fire in the waiting room at Annfield Plain. She ran onto the verandah 'with her clothes in a blaze', a

Dunston Staiths. The coal hoppers on top of the staiths seem minuscule. (Beamish Museum)

Long Boiler 1001 Class locomotive No. 1743, involved in the incident above, pictured at Consett with Sherburn Terrace in the background. (Beamish Museum)

small boy raising the alarm when seeing her. Porter Emerson took off his overcoat and used this to put out the flames. The girl suffered burns to her right arm and one side of her face, and it was reported that if not for Emerson's prompt actions she would have burned to death.[5] As the 2101 train was leaving Annfield Plain station on the night of 25 September 1900, a builder named Patterson tried to leave the train. It was believed he had been sleeping, and after opening the door of the compartment and stepping on the footboard, he slipped between the train and the platform. The guard, Whittle, was alerted, but before the train came to a stop the wheels of the last carriage and guards van went over Patterson 'almost cutting his body in two'.[6]

A fireman (of whose employ was not stated) of Leadgate called George Robert Hall took rejection in love badly on the night of 8 December 1900, shooting young Barbara Lowery in the street near her home in Black Horse Terrace, West Pelton. He fired three times, the second shot hitting her in the left breast. Miss Lowery was carried into her house for surgical treatment, meanwhile Hall ran away onto the Annfield Plain branch some ¼ mile away and put himself on the rails in front of a passenger train, which killed him. Lowery was taken to the Newcastle Infirmary, seriously hurt, but was said several days later not to be in danger of losing her life.[7]

From local reports, it is clear that the NER and their provision of services in the area was a frequent topic of conversation at council meetings. Overcrowding on trains on the Annfield Plain branch was raised at a meeting of Tanfield Urban District Council in August 1901, one man proposing that the Board of Trade be petitioned about it, and additionally the 'dangerous condition' of Shield Row station owing to lack of footbridge or subway.[8] In particular, Shield Row station, which served the large mining town of Stanley, became a hot topic.

J27 Class locomotive No. 65871 on the line. (Beamish Museum

Local tradesmen in Stanley held a meeting in September 1902 regarding the delivery of goods from Shield Row station. It was of their opinion that delivery of parcels should be free, as it was in other places; however a letter from E. F. Wilkinson, the NER's district passenger agent, said he would recommend that the NER introduce a parcel delivery service from the station but only at a cost of 1*d* for parcels up to 28lbs and 2*d* for those between 28lbs and under 56lbs. Mr J. T. Castle, chairing the meeting, said that the NER 'had placed the station at the bottom of the hill, but that was no reason why the tradesmen should suffer'. Another man said that if they could not get a satisfactory answer they should insist on an interview with the directors of the NER, and all attending decided to ask for free delivery – and also that the station name be altered to 'West Stanley'.[9]

In September 1903 a passenger and goods porter at Shield Row station called James Hume, who used the alias Butcher, was charged at Consett for stealing from the goods shed at Shield Row. Hume had been in the role for three years and had been questioned following the discovery that a kettle stand and 'tidy' which had been stored at the shed had gone missing. Hume had given the kettle stand to a woman, and the 'tidy' was found broken up in a cavity of the goods shed between the platform and crane. Hume admitted the theft and was fined 40*s*.[10] Annfield Plain station was broken into between the Sunday night and Monday morning of 27/28 March 1904 – the booking office window was prised open with platelayer's tools and the perpetrator went through numerous drawers, but did not get into the till, which contained money. Bundles of clothing on the floor of the booking

A large consignment of bananas being unloaded from a Midland Railway van at Annfield Plain, *c.* 1910. (Beamish Museum)

office were opened, and bizarrely the thief decided to tear his old suit to pieces to dress in the new clothes, leaving his old suit behind.[11]

Another theft occurred at Shield Row station on the night of 5 November 1904. Two miners, Malloss and Halpin, had come off an excursion train shortly before midnight, and picked up two parcels lying on the platform and simply walked off with them. They were seen by porter Barnes and stationmaster Windus, and the two men were stopped by PC Ferguson still with the parcels, claiming that they had picked the parcels up by mistake and had been drinking in Newcastle all day. They were fined 20*s*.[12] In August 1905 a shed at Shield Row station was broken into one night, with a lady's bicycle stolen and another parcel disturbed, but nothing else taken.[13]

In December 1905 the lack of a passenger bridge or subway at Shield Row and the existing arrangement of crossing the tracks was considered 'very dangerous' at a meeting of North West Durham urban councils at Annfield Plain, the chairman expressing surprise that the Board of Trade had not interfered already. There were also clamours for additional trains, as there was no train between the 5.24 and 9.05 p.m. from Shield Row to Newcastle, so after a discussion an agreement was made to ask the NER for an extra train to reach Newcastle at around 7.45 p.m. and to rearrange a Sunday train service – as well as provision of a subway at Shield Row station.[14]

Consett station, which consisted of an island platform accessed on foot by the road overbridge which replaced the Delves Lane level crossing. (Beamish Museum)

As a train slowed for Pelton station on 21 April 1906, deputy overman at Pelton Fell colliery, Daniel Clasper, opened the door of the carriage compartment he was in as the train reached a bridge outside Pelton station, and stood on the footboard facing the van at the end of the train. Two passengers told him not to step off until the train stopped, but he jumped off onto the platform and fell onto his back (one witness described Clasper as doing a 'complete somersault'), falling between the end of the carriage he was on and the next carriage, becoming wedged between the footboard and the platform as well as between the footboard and the springs of the carriage. Clasper was dragged 15 yards until the train stopped, with part of the footboard having to be sawn away to retrieve Clasper, dead, having suffered a dislocated neck and other injuries. Clasper's brother tried to claim that the train had stopped and then started again which had caused the accident but six witnesses testified that it had not done so.[15,16] Another death on the line three months later did not involve the railway at all, simply being the location of its occurrence – sixty-six-year-old Ambrose Gray suffered a heart attack in the booking hall at Consett station, and died instantly.[17]

Snow, which heavily affected lines in the area, stranded a goods train on the curve between Consett and Blackhill station in December 1906 despite having four engines attached, with all stations on the Annfield Plain branch then told not to book passengers for Blackhill as services would terminate at Consett and return to Newcastle when practical.[18] It was reported the next day that a passenger train from Newcastle to Consett was embedded in the snow at Greencroft, between Annfield Plain and Leadgate, the snow then stopping all traffic on the Annfield Plain branch.[19]

A train of iron ore heading towards Consett the night of 2 August 1907 met with disaster, the wagons breaking away from the engine about half a mile towards Annfield Plain from Shield Row, the thirteen wagons running back down the gradient. The guard, Sheppard, tried to stop the train with the brake van but it was insufficient to do so and he jumped clear, fortunately not injuring himself whilst doing so. At Shield Row – where the runaway was said to be travelling at about 30 mph – the signalman switched the wagons from the up line to the down line, as per regulations, so they were on the correct line, and at great speed went past Beamish. At Pelton the runaway was reckoned to be travelling at 80 mph and was outpacing the speed at which telegraph messages which were being sent from signal box to signal box warning of it. At Pelton the wagons hit a van and locomotive which were shunting, smashing the top part of the van and throwing the locomotive some yards, completely wrecking the front part of the locomotive. The guard in the brake van, William Berry, was believed to have been killed instantly, having been 'terribly mangled'.[20] The driver and fireman of the locomotive jumped clear; the driver was injured but the fireman was unscathed. The rails were torn up for a significant distance and passenger traffic was suspended until cleared.[21] The cause of the runaway was due to the breaking of the coupling, the shackle eye having been opened out at some point, presumably earlier in the day by an 'extraordinary jerk' which had also drawn out the cotter pin from one of the eyes. As the point where the runaway occurred the line was level, a platelayer mentioned that it was usual for drivers to gain extra speed on that section before the next steep gradient, so the additional 'jerk' as speed increased had 'completed the opening' of the shackle and caused it to break. The locomotive superintendent of the Northern Division of the NER mentioned he had never seen a shackle break like this before.[22]

Leadgate station with a loaded mineral train heading towards Consett. (Beamish Museum)

Shield Row station (renamed West Stanley in 1934) showing the station after the footbridge was added. (Beamish Museum)

Satisfaction regarding the crossing of tracks at Shield Row came in 1908, with the welcome news received by Stanley Urban District Council in a letter from the General Manager of the NER stating the directors had approved a scheme which included a footbridge between the two platforms and enlarging the buildings including the booking office at the station.[23] In 1910 a group of tradesmen from Stanley held a meeting with Ralph Wedgwood, NER Traffic Manager, and Mr Swainson of the Passenger Department at Newcastle regarding grievances with the NER. The tradesmen wished to have a goods station at Shield Row opened as soon as possible, with the present system of free delivery in Annfield Plain causing a delay to them getting their goods. The present use of a siding at Oxhill was 'very unsatisfactory'. From 1906 the NER had a road steam wagon service from Newcastle Forth goods station to the Stanley area, but although it offered same-day delivery from Newcastle, traffic was never high and owing to frequent breakdowns, it stopped in 1908. Wedgwood, who of course later became Chief Officer of the LNER, said the deputation of tradesmen 'had perhaps come at a fortunate time' owing to congestion at Shield Row, although a goods station there may make matters for the tradesmen worse as goods for Stanley would have to go to Annfield Plain and wait for another train to take them to Shield Row. Wedgwood agreed more accommodation was needed and would investigate how the matter could be best met. The deputation went further by asking for free delivery of passengers' parcels from Shield Row station and that it be renamed to West Stanley, with Mr Swainston promising these would receive consideration.[24]

Louisa Pit at South Moor colliery in Stanley with a Barclay 0-4-0ST shunting locomotive seen crossing the road. The original S&TR route ran the other side of the wall, which the level crossing ran off from. (Beamish Museum)

In 1910 the NER moved just over 38 million tons of coal and coke, more than any other railway (the Midland Railway followed with 26.5 million tons, then the London & North Western Railway at 21.9 million tons). In 1911, around a fifth of Britain's entire output of coal was from the Durham and Northumberland coalfields, nearly 42 million tons and nearly 15 million tons respectively, out of a total of 272 million total. Over a third of Durham and Northumberland's coal at this time was shipped abroad. An incredible 5 million tons of this was transiting via Stella Gill, 4 million tons of this mostly being shipped from Tyne Dock (which was handling over 7 million tons a year in total from around 250 collieries) with 15 per cent of it going via a slightly more awkward route, doubling back on itself to Dunston Staiths (handling around 3½ million tons of coal annually from 200 collieries). The remaining 1 million tons from Stella Gill was sold in the local area, mainly to factories. Of the coal output shipped via the Tyne, in 1911 just over a quarter was sent by coaster down to London or elsewhere in Britain; the majority – just over 15 million tons – was exported. The year 1913 was the Durham coalfields year of peak production, which consequently meant 1913 was the best year for the North Eastern Railway – 275 million tons of coal was produced in Britain that year. 1914 looked set to either beat or match it, but for the outbreak of the First World War.

Blast furnaces, hot-blast stoves and pig beds at Consett Iron Works. (Beamish Museum)

The ironworks at Consett, by now also producing steel, continued to be a large generator of traffic, not just for iron ore but similarly large amounts of coal and limestone as part of the metal-making process, and the products of the works to be shipped out. In 1912, the NER described how the works 'contain eight blast furnaces and consume 550,000 tons of iron ore yearly. The works have an annual output of a quarter of a million tons of iron and steel, the whole of which, together with the incoming ore, passes over the lines of the North Eastern Railway.' The works was on an enormous site, so to deal with the huge amounts of traffic in, out, and internally, a complex network of railway lines spread over the works, and to nearby mines and other sites associated with the works, together with running rights over NER lines. Consett traffic was also routed via the other NER lines in the area, and non-passenger traffic was not solely coal and iron/steel related. Bricks were also moved in sizeable quantities, and many collieries had coke ovens. Goods traffic handled at the stations on the line included stone, sand, loam and general goods for the population of the area. Prior to the passenger stations built after the 1893 deviation, there were goods stations at Annfield Plain and Stella Gill.

A labourer called Alexander Dutfield was charged 40*s* and costs in September 1912 for his behaviour at Annfield Plain station on 31 August. Dutfield had offered a woman in

Above: Consett Iron Company A Class locomotive No. 16, built by Hudswell Clarke in 1916. The gouge out of the buffer beam and less-than-level footplate gives an idea of their hard-working life. (Beamish Museum)

Below: Two of the Consett Iron Company's E Class cranes and an A Class locomotive seen in the Templetown sheds in August 1935. (Beamish Museum)

the waiting room £10 for her baby, and when she refused 'put his arm around her neck and indulged in abusive language'.[25] Another conviction – in this case the assailant's seventieth – occurred two years later when labourer John Johnson drunkenly assaulted stationmaster John Symons at Leadgate station on 27 June 1914. Johnson was said to have been so violent that the stationmaster had to find a cord and tie Johnson to the parcel office desk to restrain him until the police arrived, and whilst doing so Johnson tried to bite Symons' ear. At the hearing Johnson said he knew nothing about it other than the stationmaster striking him several times! Johnson was committed to prison for one month with hard labour.[26]

At the quarterly meeting of Durham County Council in early 1913, Councillor Bulmer of Annfield Plain inadvertently raised laughter during a complaint of overcrowding of passenger trains on the line. The councillor described how there were thirteen people in the carriage compartment with him so pulled the communication cord (which, applying the through-train brake, alerts the guard and engine crew that there is an issue) which resulted in the stationmaster, guard and other staff to come 'running up as though some convicts had escaped from Durham Gaol'. Bulmer also added that overcrowding led to disease. In a light-hearted response, the councillor was asked what the fine was for pulling the cord – Bulmer responding that it was £5![27] In February 1913, a letter from the NER was read out at a meeting of Stanley Urban District Council regarding the council's request to rename Shield Row station to 'Stanley', or failing that, 'West Stanley'. The NER mentioned that as there were eight other places in County Durham named Stanley, changing the name would cause confusion. The council decided to call the attention of the NER to the proposed name of West Stanley, which as far as they knew would not clash with any other places they were aware of and would also remove the confusion caused by the existing name. In general, the passenger service was locally considered unsatisfactory, and in the council's view the current Newcastle to Blackhill service was 'altogether inadequate for the traffic on the line'. In response, the NER told the council they could not meet the council's request to run an hourly service between Newcastle and Blackhill.[28]

With there being a passenger station on the line at South Shields, a goods station at West Boldon, and a passenger station at Washington on the Leamside line adjacent to the P&SSR line, there were repeated calls for a passenger service linking them and with the wider service in North East Durham; indeed, it may seem strange that there was not a passenger service along the entire P&SSR route by this stage. In 1914, however, the NER responded that the sheer amount of mineral traffic ruled against this.

The new goods station at Shield Row was announced in early 1914 to be opened on 2 March. Cartage service had been arranged and full truck loads for the Shield Row area would continue to be dealt with at Shield Row station, but smaller consignments of general goods traffic to and from the area would be carted from and to Shield Row goods station.[29]

Two young boys were fined *6s 6d* each at Consett Police Court in August 1915 following being charged with trespassing on railway property on 20 August. The boys had 'annoyed the passengers leaving the trains' at Shield Row station, offering to carry parcels, with the passengers considering them a nuisance and complaining about them.[30] Even in time of war, Shield Row station's title was a cause of complaint, described as 'that omnipotent grievance of the name of Stanley's railway station'. It was reported in August 1915 that although the issue was certain to be raised in the Stanley Council elections in the following

Electric conveyer for loading coal into ships at Tyne Dock in NER days. (Beamish Museum)

March, it had also been mentioned at the annual banquet of the Irish Institute. It was recognised that although other railway stations had the name Stanley, the recent opening of the goods station being called Stanley (which had 'doubtless minimised some of the inconvenience formerly caused to tradesmen') showed that the same thing should apply in the case of the passenger station.[31]

Coal teemers at Tyne Dock. They would open the doors on hopper wagons to drop out the coal into ships being loaded. (Beamish Museum)

Tragically a female porter on the NER, Beatrice Ogden of New Kyo, was killed whilst crossing the tracks at Annfield Plain station, where she was employed, on the night of 18 January 1917. She was knocked down by a passenger train from Consett, dying of severe head injuries. Ogden's husband was stated as being a prisoner of war in Germany at the time.[32] The following month a young woman, a widow to a soldier killed some months before, was run over by a passenger train from Blackhill to Newcastle near Pelton station. She had been reported as being 'in a melancholy condition' since her husband's death.[33] During the First World War, at least one extra service was put on the line, the 5.55 p.m. workmen's train from Consett via Birtley to Newcastle for munitions workers (it is worth mentioning that although not strictly included in this book, although services ran to the station, Birtley was home to thousands of refugee Belgians during the war – the 'Birtley Belgians' – who worked a munitions works there). A letter was published by the *Newcastle Daily Chronicle* in November 1918 with the writer wanting to call the NER's attention not to stop this service now 'that the war is practically over' as it had become popular with the general public too, and to extend the 5.15 p.m. from Newcastle that terminated at Annfield Plain to instead carry on to Consett and return, perhaps in place of the workmen's train. The anonymous writer considered that to 'the residents of the Consett district these are train reforms now long overdue'.[34] Despite the popularity of the passenger services on the P&SSR, and frequent calls for them to be expanded, before the service was thirty years old it would go into decline.

CHAPTER 5

The Pontop Inclines

The remaining three inclined planes on the P&SSR route, the Pontop inclines of Stanley, Eden Hill and Waldridge, remained busy, even with the opening of the deviation. This was due to the amount of coal traffic to be moved, which had grown to tremendous proportions, from the Annfield Plain and Stanley area and traffic joining the inclines along the route, with Twizell colliery joining at the head of Eden Hill incline, and substantial traffic joining on the Pelton Level from the Burnhope waggonway.

The method of operating the inclines by the early twentieth century was likely identical to how they had operated since 1834, other than the rails now being of long steel lengths and on wooden sleepers rather than the original short 'fishbelly' iron rails on stone sleeper

Two sets of P7 20-ton hoppers crossing on the Stanley incline in LNER days. (*The Railway Magazine*)

blocks, and the wagons being hopper wagons of varying capacities (usually of 10-, 10.5- or 20-ton capacity) rather than the chaldrons which carried just over 2½ tons. By the 1900s, a 'set' travelling over the inclines was usually of four to six hoppers, with one set travelling each way, passing in the middle. The operation was controlled by the brakesman, in a cabin at the incline head. The brakesman operated a wheel which, via a rod, operated the brake on the brake wheel at the top of the incline. The rope ran around the brake wheel, which was made of cast iron and 15 feet and 9 inches in diameter. It was placed in a chamber underneath the track, a sufficient distance away from the head of the incline so that it was more than the maximum set's length away from the crest of the incline.

Next to the brake wheel, again underneath the tracks in a chamber, was a smaller-diameter binding wheel. By having the rope go around the binding wheel, this ensured it went around more of the circumference of the brake wheel, which would prevent it slipping. The binding wheel was slightly tilted to one side so that the rope did not foul on itself between the binding and brake wheel where it crossed over itself. The lower periphery of the brake wheel had grooved timber bolted onto it which the rope ran over rather than on the wheel

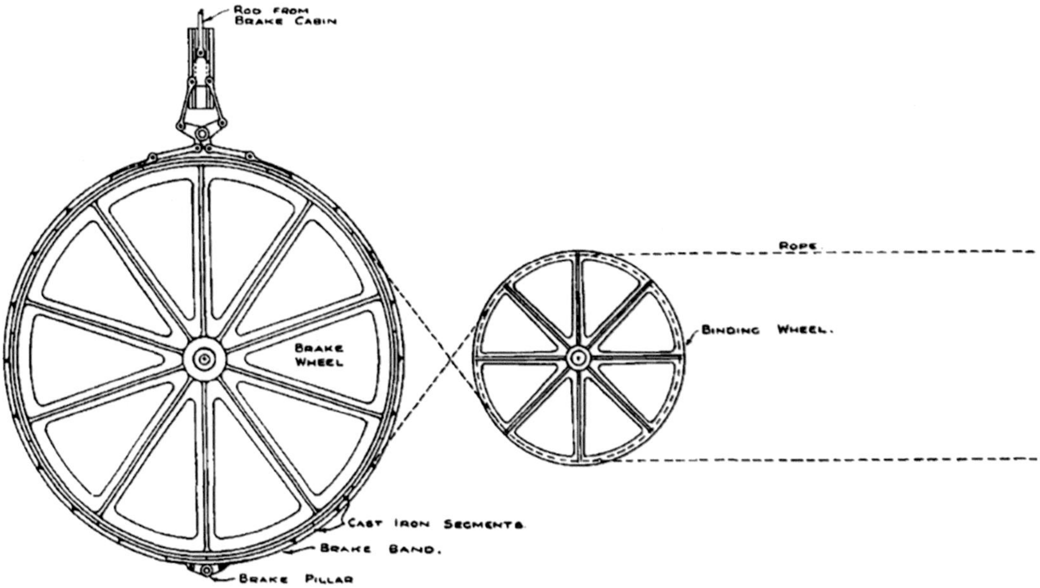

Plan view of the brake wheel, showing the rod from the brake cabin and the smaller binding wheel.

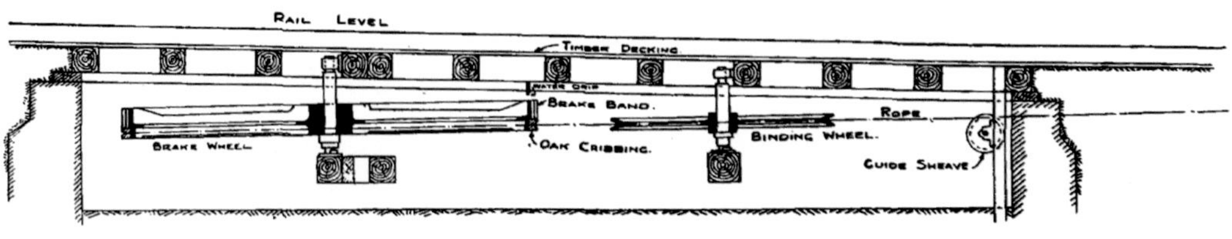

Side view of the brake wheel pit.

itself, and on the outside of the brake wheel, cast-iron replaceable segments were attached, coming into contact with brake blocks replaced every three months (in 1898), fixed to an iron band brake made of two semi-circular sections. The braking caused a lot of friction, so a jet of water was constantly run over the wheel rim to keep the temperature down. Except for emergencies, all braking on the inclines was done by the brakesman from the cabin rather than the bankrider. The responsibility of the brakesman was a heavy one, having to regulate the speed of traffic for it to be safe but also ensure a steady rate, and take into account weather conditions. Another factor affecting the running would be the occasional change in gradient of the inclines caused by mining subsidence which caused wagons starting to suddenly accelerate where they hadn't before, where new dips in the track occurred. Owing to the distances involved in daytime, and especially so at night and in poor visibility conditions such as fog, the brakesman used the sound of the sets with a well-honed ear from years of experience to regulate the speed of the sets. In 1898, the transit time for a set of wagons on the Stanley incline was about six to eight minutes to cover its length of $1\frac{1}{3}$ miles.

The top third of the incline consisted of two tracks, one for uphill traffic and one for downhill traffic, but sharing a central rail, so there would be three rails for two sets of line. The use of two tracks but with a central rail obviously meant sets could not pass each other along it, but it was done so that the rope for the set on the lower part of the incline was clear of the set on the upper part of the incline. At the middle portion of the incline, the tracks diverged into two fully separate tracks. This middle portion was called the 'meeting' as it was where the two sets met each other, passing on this section. Below the meeting, the lower third of the incline was single track, as a set travelling on this part of the line would not have the rope for the other set alongside it.

Men in front of an NER P4 10.5-ton hopper at Waldridge Bank Foot or Stella Gill. One of the men holds the lock chain quoit pin used to attach the hopper wagons to the incline rope – the bankriders' years of experience make them the best judge of when to kick it off. (Beamish Museum)

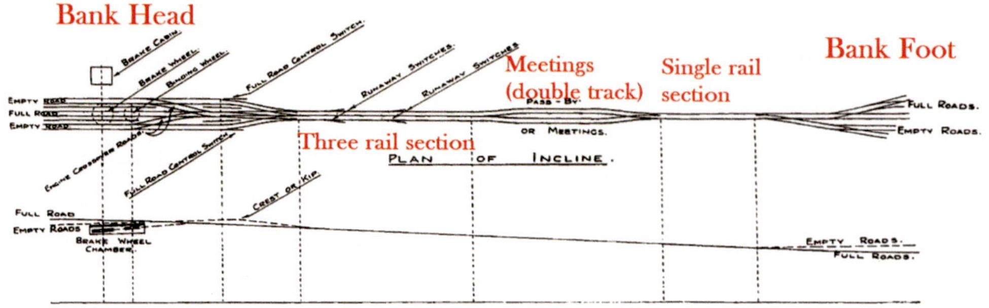

Explanatory diagram of a self-acting incline.

The ropes used on the inclines were, at first, made of India rubber solution. The S&TR found these became soft and swollen in wet weather, which made them unsuitable, particularly with the friction the ropes would receive whilst being worked. They were changed for ropes made of hemp, which were sometimes protected by being tarred to reduce wear, and gave them a smooth, shiny appearance. Despite this, the ropes would usually last just seven months, and rarely more than ten months, and more durable wire ropes were starting to come into use by the time the P&SSR was formed. The cost of working the self-acting inclines was calculated by the S&TR in 1839 as £415 per mile which, despite the lack of mechanical power used in their operation, was just £70 cheaper than the hardest-working stationary engine worked incline. In the early years of the line, collieries tended to have idle periods in the New Year, with the railway taking the opportunity to close the line for a week to undertake overhauls of the inclines and their machinery.

By the early twentieth century, the rope was 1-inch thick and made of steel wire, and by 1898 was averaging a life of seventeen months, rising to two years by 1923 – one rope was remarked as working 71,613 sets before replacement, the equivalent of over 80,000 miles. At the end of the rope, the wire strands were turned over and held in a riveted socket, which was then attached to a 20-foot-long chain. To attach this onto the wagon at the end of the set, there was a separate short chain consisting of three links. The first link went onto the wagon's coupling hook, and the third link had a lock chain, a metal casting which was roughly P shaped. This went through the final link on the chain at the end of the incline rope, linking the two chains together, then came back on itself towards the wagon, with a quoit between the lock chain and middle link secured by a cotter pin.

Each set of wagons had a bankrider, and to detach the rope from the set at the end of its journey along the incline, the bankrider took out the cotter pin and kicked the quoit, which would open the end of the lock chain, which meant the chain (attached to the rope) would detach and fall to the ground.

The head of Waldridge incline, the busiest of the three Pontop inclines owing to the collieries joining the route on the Pelton level, had three separate tracks at its head owing to the heavier traffic. The two outer lines were on raised 'kips', which after reaching the incline head had a slight hump, then a declining gradient away from the incline, to help prevent wagons running back down the incline. These were used for the empty sets coming back uphill. The loaded sets were started from the central road, which had a downhill

Above: Looking down the three-rail section near the top of Eden Hill incline. In the distance the two sets of hoppers can be seen passing, the rope for each set visible on the rollers. (*The Railway Magazine*)

Below: Diagram of the lock chain used on the Pontop inclines.

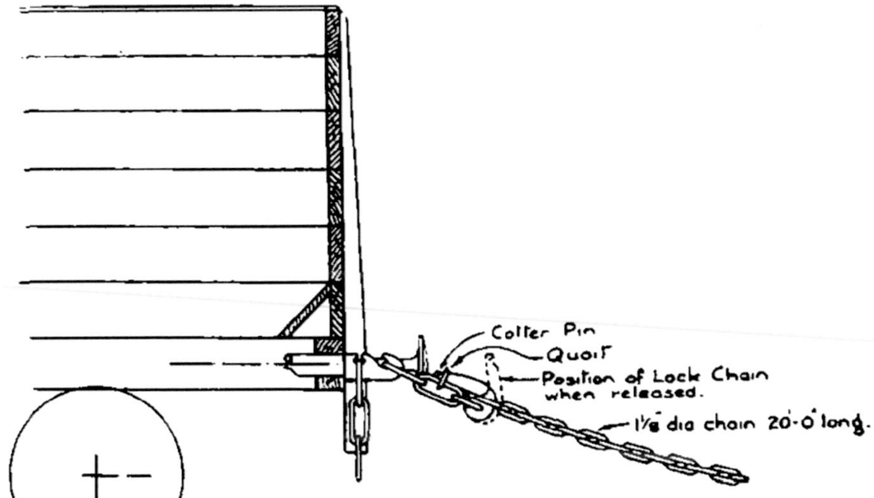

gradient towards the incline so that when the brakes were released, they would begin to descend the incline automatically.

When a set of wagons at the bottom (foot) of the incline was attached to the rope and ready for travelling along it, the bankrider would wind up the 'token' wire using a winch alongside the incline. Raising the wire raised a weighted indicator at the head of the incline and rang a bell in the brakesman's cabin also at the head, therefore giving both a visual and audible signal that they were ready to leave. A telephone had been added by the 1920s between the brake cabins on the Pontop inclines for further communication. When the set of wagons at the head of the incline was ready to go too, the brakesman would wind up the winch at his end, the head of the incline, which lowered the weight and the 'token' wire, showing to the incline foot that the sets were about to move. This simple method, barely if at all changed since 1834, also provided a form of emergency communication. If anything went wrong along the incline, the wire, which ran alongside it, could be pulled (which would mean a bankrider getting off the set, or someone else using it) to give an indication to the brakesman that something was wrong, and they could apply the brake as much as possible – it also meant those at the incline foot could set the 'catch' points which would intentionally derail wagons, and otherwise do what they could to minimise the potential damage if there was a runaway set of wagons coming their way.

Brake cabin at the head of Eden Hill incline, with a P7 20-ton hopper on the line to Twizell colliery on the right. There looks to be a horseshoe on the wall of the brake cabin above the head of the person on the left – perhaps for 'good luck'. The original was destroyed in the 1894 runaway of twenty wagons down the Stanley incline, and this is the replacement. (Beamish Museum)

Although self-acting for most of their life, an account in 1899 by William Teasdale, a contractor responsible for permanent way and operation on the Stanhope & Tyne and later the P&SSR, mentions use of stationary engine for assisting iron ore wagons up towards the ironworks at Consett. He describes 'when the haematite iron ore began to be imported at Tyne Dock, it was found impossible to raise the enormous quantity of iron ore over the upper part of the Stanley incline by the self-acting arrangements, the momentum of the descending train being insufficient to haul up the ore trucks. A stationary engine, which had afterwards to be doubled, was consequently arranged at the top to assist the ascending load'.

The 6-inch-to-the-mile map of the area surveyed in 1857 and published in 1861 describes the bank top of Stanley as 'Stanley Engine' and shows a building adjacent to the incline which could be a winding house. Certainly, by the 1850s locomotives were fitted with longer-axle boxes enabling them to work on the inclines too, presumably in assisting sets of loaded wagons, such as iron ore trains for Consett, up the inclines. The Stanley engine was no doubt soon taken out of service after the opening of the 1893 deviation, the building marked the Stanley Engine having gone in the 1895 revision showing just the brake cabin at the bank head.

In 1898 the average number of sets running over the Stanley inclines for the three years previous was 426 sets a week, carrying 26,838 tons of coal, amounting to around 1.4 million tons per year. The cost to the NER was £1,050 a year just for the Stanley incline, the main

Staff of the Pontop inclines: brakesmen Dinning, Curry, Grievson, Finlay, Welsh and Dunn (left to right) on the back row, with Inspector Bone central in the front row flanked by Sub-Inspectors Siddle (left) and Sanderson (right).

cost being the wages for the six men working it including overtime (£520), maintenance of the incline equipment i.e. ropes and sheaves (£350), maintenance of permanent way and the interest on the first cost of the incline (£180). By early 1923, the maximum gross load per set of loaded wagons heading downhill along the Pontop inclines was 116 tons on the Stanley and Eden Hill inclines and 174 tons on the Waldridge incline. In the six months previous, 1½ million tons of coal had passed on the Waldridge incline, and recently during a single eight-hour shift sixty-one sets, carrying 7,000 tons of coal, had come down the Waldridge incline in a single shift, meaning very little interval in between runs. There would also be some lighter miscellaneous traffic heading uphill using the empty sets going to the collieries in the area. Testament to the men on the inclines came from NER Chief Engineer Charles A. Harrison in 1898:

> The men employed on the inclines, at any rate on those owned by the North Eastern Railway Company, are *sui generis,* as not only they but their fathers and grandfathers were brakesmen, bankriders and inclinemen before them. If anything goes wrong with the working they are perfectly competent to find out the cause and remedy the defect. They renew the brakes when required, splice the ropes if a defective strand is detected, and in every way take a pride that their particular incline should be worked properly. In all weathers (and there are 'weathers' on those hill-sides) they ride their wagons contentedly, and there is no grade in the employment of the North Eastern Railway who work better and more pleasantly than the men on the self-acting inclines.

A Midland Railway wagon at Stella Gill. (Beamish Museum)

Ralph Mowbray, a bankrider on the Waldridge incline, was fatally injured on 11 January 1893 whilst uncoupling empty hoppers. Mowbray had not uncoupled properly, and the rope dragged him against a buffer, causing fatal injuries. This led to an inquiry and report by the Board of Trade. The result of the report was that it was due to a mistake by Mowbray, Major Marindin who investigated the accident and completed the report, stating: 'No one was in a position to save him from the consequences of his mistake, and no person is to blame for what occurred.' Although Mowbray had only been on duty a short amount of time, the inquiry looked at the working hours of men on the incline as they were considered excessive. Although Mowbray had only been on duty for fifteen minutes since he started at 6 a.m., his previous duty, which ended at 9.50 p.m. the previous night, had been fifteen hours and fifty minutes long.

The further inquiry found cause for issue with the working hours of men on the inclines. From 28 November to 4 February, the busiest time of year, the average shift time was fourteen hours and forty-one minutes, and without stoppages the actual average daily hours worked was nine hours and five minutes. The working day was fixed at eleven hours, from 6 a.m. to 5 p.m., with an hour for meals and any additional hours paid as overtime. It was usual for work to carry on for as long as there was traffic to be sent down the inclines, the only limit being that work had to stop at midnight for three days of the week, and at nine o'clock on other days, but after Mowbray's accident, orders were given that work was never to continue past ten at night. The NER had offered to reduce the hours by having two shifts, but the men unanimously asked for no change to be made, having already got the NER to agree to reduce the working day from twelve hours down to eleven. Major Marindin who conducted the report found that the men were 'thoroughly contented with their lot, and it was most satisfactory to hear the terms in which they spoke of their employers'. Marindin considered that it was 'very undesirable' to take further action which would affect the harmony on this part of the NER. Marindin's comments on the work of bankriders on the inclines makes for interesting reading and goes some way to explaining why the working of the inclines changed so little over the years:

> The work performed by the bank-riders has the appearance of being of a dangerous character, and no doubt it would be so to an inexperienced man, but these men have a very long training, commencing when quite young, and many of them, I understand, succeeded to their fathers or other relations, and this accident is the first of the kind on record, although one bank-rider was killed about twelve years ago, when trying to get up at the middle of a train of empties after it had started, which he ought not to have attempted to do so.
>
> I would have thought that a better and safer mode of uncoupling than that in force might easily have been devised, but all the men are averse to any change, although they have frequently been asked if they could suggest any improvement, and I hesitate, therefore, to suggest that any alteration should be made in a system with which all those interested have been familiar for years.

Despite the wish to keep the single shift, by early 1923 there were two shifts being worked, with sixty-six men in total, including those at work at Walridge incline foot, staffing the Pontop inclines.

Louisa Pit in Stanley with a Black Hawthorn saddle tank shunter visible. (Beamish Museum)

An accident in 1894 on the Stanley incline was believed to have been the worst accident on the Pontop inclines (described as such in early 1923, so may have later been superseded!). A rake of thirty-two wagons was sat at the top of the incline when a locomotive buffered up to them, ready for coupling and taking away. The wagons had not been properly secured, and the slight nudge of the locomotive was sufficient to get them moving and head back down the incline. Reaching a colossal speed, they hit a dozen wagons sat at the bottom of Stanley incline/Eden Hill bank top, and destroyed the brake cabin for Eden Hill incline, resulting in a high pile of wrecked wagons.

Similarly on 28 December 1903, a set of six hoppers ran down the Stanley incline and hit a set of empties at Eden Hill bank top with a breakdown gang at work all the following day to clear away the debris, although it did not interrupt the traffic on the inclines. A set of 20-ton hoppers ran away down the Eden Hill incline on 20 April 1922, smashing up at the foot of the incline and blocking the line, requiring several hours work from a breakdown gang until it was cleared. There were other near misses. In one instance, a short distance after starting their descent, the front wagons broke away from the last wagon of a set of loaded wagons heading down the Waldridge incline. The bankrider, J. Welsh, was on this last wagon, which was attached to the rope, and he chased the runaways on foot after they passed the runaway points. Welsh was able to climb over the wagons from the rear to the front, pinning down all the brakes and bringing them to a stop. Bankrider Armin had commenced heading down Eden Hill incline with a loaded set when he realised, after the

Men with long service on the Pontop inclines, totalling 270 years' service, taken at the time of retirement of Mr Hutton *c.* early 1923. Left to right: J. Hutton, J. Curry (retired), J. Welsh (retired), T. Dunn and W. Curry. This appears to be Eden Hill incline bank top, showing the replacement brake cabin on the right after the destruction of the previous in the 1894 runaway. The line to Twizell colliery is on the right behind the cabin. (Beamish Museum)

wagons had passed the runaway switches and at the point he would usually climb onto the wagons for the descent, that there was no empty set attached to the other end of the rope. Like Welsh he climbed from one wagon to another pinning all brakes down, but they reached too high a speed and were derailed on runaway switches at the bottom of the incline. Armin was able to detach the rope before jumping off, reducing the risk of further damage from the rope lashing around. Trespass was also an issue on the Pontop inclines, as elsewhere. In 1901 a man was on the Stanley incline 'in the act of flying pigeons' when Police Constable Whitfield had to pull the man out of the way of an approaching set of wagons. The man was fined 10*s.*[1]

CHAPTER 6

The Changing Railway

Although it was strongly considered by the residents along the line from Pelton to Consett that more passenger services were required, from 1921 passenger numbers on the branch went into rapid decline. The growth of motor bus services which could better serve the numerous pit villages and towns in the area became more popular, with Shield Row going from 138,664 passengers booked in 1920 to 89,760 in 1921, and it was a similar pattern elsewhere. Adding to the woes of declining receipts on the line, a fire at Annfield Plain station in July 1925 caused a 'large portion' of the station to be destroyed, with the waiting room, porters' room and coal house gutted. Although the signalman, J. Hodgson, spotted the flames and raised the alarm, the fire brigade attended quickly and were aided by other railway staff and volunteer helpers, it still took two hours to put out all the flames on the largely wooden building. It was believed that a spark from a passing train caused the fire, which was believed to have caused £300–£400 worth of damage.[1] In later years the wooden-built signal box at Annfield East junction where the 1893 and 1886 deviations met burnt down and was replaced with a brick-built signal box. Given how hard engines would be working uphill to Consett, it is not overly surprising that lineside fires were a danger on the line.

The North Eastern Railway became part of the London & North Eastern Railway (LNER) in 1923, following the Grouping, leading to gradual changes to locomotive and rolling stock liveries, station colours and staff uniform. The engine of the passenger service from Newcastle to Consett on the evening of 27 August 1927 suffered a broken driving rod when between Annfield Plain and Leadgate. The engine then 'went amain for some distance' but the driver and fireman were able to stop it, and no one was hurt. The breakdown train arrived just after midnight, although chaos soon ensued as the engine of the breakdown train hit the damaged engine, causing it to run away for 'a considerable distance before stopping'. The railway was damaged for 40 to 50 yards owing to broken and displaced rails and sleepers, and the line was reduced to single working, causing delays into the next morning. By three that afternoon the line was back to double-line working.[2]

The Waldridge incline was used for the marking of the centenary of the Stanhope & Tyne on 10 September 1934. The deputy chairman of the LNER, Sir Murrough J. Wilson

Tyne Dock in the 1930s. Owing to the reduction in the coal trade, one of the four coal staiths had been removed down to water level. (Kind Courtesy of Malcolm Charlton, not to be reused)

KBE, together with other railway officials and various sightseers, watched a set of wagons pass up and down the incline, and unveiled a tablet marking the centenary. A number of retired workers attended and a former brakesman, W. Curry, presented the deputy chairman with a chromium-plated model of the lock chain used on the inclines, made by the staff at the LNER Signal & Telegraph shops at York.

The economic downturn of the 1930s saw the LNER looking to save costs where possible, and a report in July 1939 pointed out that the Pontop inclines were expensive to operate in terms of manpower, maintenance, and locomotive working on the Pelton level, as well as shunting at either end. It was recommended to close the Stanley and Eden Hill inclines (Twizell colliery, at the head of the Eden Hill incline, closed in 1938, so there was no need to move traffic from it), and halve the hours of operation on the Waldridge incline from sixteen to eight hours a day, so the collieries reached by it could still be served. The collieries in Stanley could still be served using the 1893 deviation. This would save £7,000 a year, although it was offset by increased locomotive working over the deviation and related improvements, i.e. signalling and telephone facilities, but overall they still saved £5,000 a year. The report also recommended expanding the shed at Consett and closing Annfield Plain shed. The Stanley and Eden Hill inclines stayed open until 1946 owing to the war, but Annfield Plain shed closed in 1940. The line running on a high embankment, then into a deep cutting just west of Beamish station where the line passes through Hell Hole Wood, was considerably at risk of landslide. These fears came true early on the morning of 21 January 1939. Owing to heavy rain and snow, for the previous week men had walked the line regularly day and night for

Washington station in British Railways days. The station was on the Leamside line, but the goods lines in the background are the P&SSR route. (Beamish Museum)

any signs of problems. A walker patrolling at 5.30 a.m. that day had shown everything to be fine. Fifteen minutes later, however, signalman Robert Walker came across a landslide between 12 and 16 feet deep, and for a distance of 30 to 40 yards. Walker rarely walked to work on the line, but fortuitously he did so on that day. After discovering the landslide, he climbed over it and ran the mile to Beamish signal box in time to stop the 6.05 a.m. passenger train from Newcastle from coming across it in heavy rain and thick fog, which meant it may not have stopped in time. Walker, in the signal box, refused to be interviewed when a reporter from the *Newcastle Evening Chronicle* went to Beamish station later that day. Although Walker was lauded in the newspapers across the country for his actions, stationmaster Mallon was fairly nonchalant about the issue, saying to the reporter that had Walker not discovered the landslide the line walker would have done on his return journey and could have raised warning in time to stop the train. Whilst repair gangs from Newcastle and elsewhere worked to clear a single line, trains from Blackhill terminated at West Stanley and those from Newcastle at Beamish, with a bus running between the two to convey passengers and goods. Reportedly, local residents 'on hearing of the landslide, immediately thought of sabotage, bearing in mind I.R.A. activities'.[3]

Just two years later there was another landslip at Hell Hole Wood, after a series of heavy snowstorms during February 1941 and then a thaw at the month's end. The trackbed and

Sir Murrough J. Wilson KBE unveiling a plaque at Waldridge incline marking the centenary of the S&TR. Fortunately it still survives, in the collection at Darlington North Road Station Museum. (Beamish Museum)

Beamish station with a V1/3 Class 2-6-2T heading to Consett. (Beamish Museum)

An LNER poster advertising the services available at Tyne Dock. (Beamish Museum)

the land above slipped on the morning of 4 March, with the track covered up to 30 feet deep for a length of 30 yards. A J39 Class locomotive, No. 1577, and a brake van were running from Stanley down the line towards Tyne Dock and did not spot the landslip until too late. With the land beneath subsiding, No. 1577 and the brake van fell down the embankment, landing 45 feet below the height of the rails and 70 feet away from the line, fortunately without serious injury to the crew or guard.

The Second World War saw the return of air raids over the North East, except this time by aeroplane instead of airship as in the First World War. Again, with staff leaving for military service, women workers joined the railway in large numbers to make up some of the shortfall. The danger faced by coastal shipping meant coal traffic instead often had to travel long distances by rail rather than being sent from Tyne Dock by ship. Coupled with the increased demand for coal, this put further strain on the line. The planned closure of the Stanley and Eden Hill inclines was pushed back until after the war, likely for these reasons. An air raid by over 100 German aircraft on the night of 9/10 April 1941 took place at the same time as there were 300 ammunition wagons being loaded at Tyne Dock. Ten wagons were set on fire, and bullets started to fly in all directions. Driver J. Steel coupled his locomotive onto the burning wagons and pulled them to the nearest water column to put out the fire. In all, six men worked from 1 a.m. to 6 a.m., despite bombs still falling nearby, and most of the ammunition was saved. Driver J. Steel, together with Inspector R. Hume, received the George Medal, with shunter J. Angus, Yard Inspector C. Colthorpe, guard R. S. Ward and assistant traffic agent G. Brown all receiving the British Empire Medal. Signalman Clark stayed in position at Tyne Dock Bottom signal box all night too, right in the centre of the bombing.

A J26 or J27 Class locomotive being lifted back onto the line after an accident. (Beamish Museum)

The pressures of the war didn't do anything to disrupt the intermittent runaways down the line, with the brakes failing on Q6 Class locomotive No. 2286 in April 1942 whilst it was at the head of a loaded coal train to the east of Annfield Plain. It gathered speed and rushed down the line for around 6 miles until it derailed at South Pelaw junction, the locomotive turning onto its side and killing the engine crew, driver M. Ridley and fireman W. Stanley. The rest of the train was wrecked, although the guard was unhurt.

The state of the railways at the end of the Second World War meant that organisational changes were needed, and the majority were nationalised in 1948, forming British Railways. In the post-war recovery period, difficult decisions had to be made regarding Britain's enormous, and expensive, railway network. Although in 1929 there were twelve trains per weekday from Newcastle to either Blackhill or Consett with nine returning to Newcastle, in the following years the number of trains started to decline to match falling passenger numbers (passenger numbers at Shield Row in 1930 were just under a quarter of 1921 numbers), with seven from Newcastle to Blackhill or Consett and eight returning by 1941, although excursion trains to the coast or even to London remained very popular. With passenger numbers continuing to fall after the Second World War, by 1951 there were just four westbound passenger trains and three eastbound a day, with an extra Saturday service each way. Like other lines in the area, closure of passenger services soon beckoned. Beamish station closed in September 1953 to passengers, Pelton following three months

Q6 Class locomotive storming through Beamish. (Beamish Museum)

Robert Stephenson & Co. 1891-built locomotive No. 3 *Twizell*, originally built for the Beamish Waggonway but later worked at other locations near the P&SSR route. It is now on long-term loan from Beamish Museum to the Tanfield Railway. (Beamish Museum)

later. The stations at Annfield Plain, Leadgate and Consett remained open to passengers until the final passenger service from Newcastle via Consett to Blackhill on 23 May 1955, hauled by V1 Class 2-6-2T No. 67657. This was also the last passenger service to Blackhill, which had lost the passenger service from the Darlington (via Tow Law, Crook and Bishop Auckland) and Durham (via Lanchester) directions in 1939, and Newcastle via the Derwent Valley line in 1954 – although these last two remained open for goods for longer.

Above: K1 Class 2-6-0 on a goods train passing East Castle heading towards Consett, on the section of line doubled in 1896. (Kind courtesy of Matthew Oliphant, not to be reused)

Below: Q6 Class locomotive at Consett heading towards the ironworks. There appears to be iron or steel sheets on wagons on the left, presumably products of the ironworks. (Beamish Museum)

CHAPTER 7

The Final Years

Iron ore to Consett was, in the immediate post-war period, handled in the 21-ton steel hoppers introduced by the LNER – essentially a modernised version of the wooden P7 20-ton hoppers introduced by the NER in the 1900s. Sir Vincent Raven's powerful three-cylinder Q7 eight-coupled locomotives handled this traffic, usually hauling twenty-two wagons with a brake van to the rear, and another Q7 or other locomotive banking from Tyne Dock and from South Pelaw up the steep gradient towards Consett.

An increase in the size of the steelworks at Consett saw British Railways, Consett Iron Company and the Tyne Improvement Company partner to solve the problem of getting the increase in iron ore from ship to steelworks, a doubling from around half a million

J39 Class locomotive on a train of 21-ton hoppers. (Beamish Museum)

tons a year to a million tons or more. New dockside facilities for unloading the ore were needed, and increased capacity wagons for moving it. Thirty distinctive 56-ton iron ore double-bogie wagons were built at Shildon with two doors on each side (rather than unloading through doors which would drop the contents between the rails as per the steel hoppers and older designs). The doors were opened by compressed air, controlled by the driver of the train, which meant locomotives which hauled the hoppers would need to be fitted with air pumps. Continuous vacuum brakes were fitted too to give control over the heavy load – even when empty the wagons weighed 28 tons and 19cwt. In 1954, iron ore was being sent in these from Tyne Dock at two-hourly intervals, with trains of eight bogie ore wagons owing to the weight and the steep climb up to Consett. In 1956, ten iron ore trains were leaving Tyne Dock a day. To give an idea of the amount of traffic to and from Consett, by the mid-1950s, 62,000 tons was arriving there a week, with 15,500 tons of product leaving. The location of the ironworks, and its reliance for most of its existence on foreign imported iron ore, meant the movement of materials to and from Consett was lengthy, and expensive. Consideration had often been given to relocating the works, or having an ore terminal at Derwenthaugh on the Tyne, which would greatly reduce the mileage for iron ore trains, but this never took place.

Amongst the first locomotives to work the traffic were Tyne Dock's allocation of five O1 Class 2-8-0 locomotives designed by Edward Thompson, rebuilds from the Great Central Railway's O4 Class. They were each fitted with two Westinghouse air pumps and vacuum ejectors, as were some of the War Department-built Austerity 2-8-0 locomotives. Five Q7s were also fitted with Westinghouse pumps for the traffic and continued to be used as

Q7 Class locomotive fitted with air pumps for working the Consett iron ore trains. (Beamish Museum)

bankers. From 1956 ten of British Railways' new Standard 9F 2-10-0 locomotives were used for the traffic, receiving the pumps from older locomotives replaced from this work. The 9Fs became the steam locomotive most associated with this work, although Q7s remained in use until the late 1950s and O1s until 1962. The powerful 9Fs could work nine loaded wagons if another 9F was available as banker from South Pelaw, if not, another locomotive was used, the ninth wagon remaining unloaded to allow for the difference in power.

Diesel locomotives started to be used as bankers in the 1960s, although steam continued owing to lack of diesels fitted with air pumps. This changed when air compressors were fitted to the Sulzer Type 2 diesels, later known as Class 24s, which tended to work the traffic in pairs. With these now available, the last steam-hauled ore train to Consett ran on 19 November 1966 with 9F No. 92063 suitably smartened for the occasion and with plenty of photographers on hand to record the day.

A new source of traffic joined the line with a siding laid to the Ransome & Marles bearings factor in 1953 at Greencroft, west of Annfield Plain, but the decline in general goods traffic on the Annfield Plain branch meant the service was removed in the early 1960s other than at Consett, which continued for some years. The Waldridge and Sacriston waggonways which ran from Stella Gill closed in 1955, although some additional traffic came to the Waldridge incline when the National Coal Board laid a short line from Handen Hold to the Pelton Level to allow traffic from the Beamish colliery to reach the Waldridge incline, and move via Stella Gill. This saw the closure of part of the Beamish Waggonway, which the original S&TR had hoped to buy before having to build their own line.

9F Class locomotive with a train of 56-ton wagons being loaded at Tyne Dock. (Beamish Museum)

Train of iron ore storming away from Tyne Dock. (Kind courtesy of Roy Lambeth, not to be reused)

Iron ore train at South Pelaw. (Kind courtesy of Roy Lambeth, not to be reused)

Iron ore train at Annfield Plain, heading on to the 1886 deviation with the original 1834 route on the left. (Beamish Museum)

This new line only stayed in use until 1966 when the Beamish pit closed. The last known incident on the inclines was that of five loaded wagons running away down the Waldridge incline in June 1966, the bankrider, sixty-three-year-old John Jackson, staying on the wagons until they reached the foot of the incline, by which time of course they had reached a high speed. At the incline foot he kicked out the holding pin to free the wire rope from the set to prevent it creating damage and potential injury to any staff nearby, then jumped clear himself before the wagons derailed, breaking his wrist, badly crushing his ribs and receiving cuts and bruising to his face and back. Arthur Dean, General Manager of the North Eastern Region of British Railways, came to Newcastle on 31 August 1966 to award Jackson £25 for gallantry. The last pit served by the Waldridge incline, that at Handen Hold, closed in 1969, and with it the Waldridge incline.[1] This was the last inclined plane in use on the Stanhope & Tyne following the closures of the Weatherhill and Crawley engine-worked inclines on the western half of the S&TR in 1951.

Splendid view of '398' Class 0-6-0 No. 815, built by Robert Stephenson & Co. in 1873, at Tyne Dock No. 1 Hole (No. 1 Bank behind) on 19 March 1895. Left to right are: Driver Ralph Charlton, Fireman T. Jewitt and Guard G. Smith. (Kind courtesy of Malcolm Charlton, not to be reused)

9F No. 92097 in unusually clean condition on the RCTS North Eastern No. 2 Rail Tour near Annfield Plain on 10 April 1965. (Kind courtesy of Roy Lambeth, not to be reused)

Class 25 diesel locomotive D5181 returning empty iron ore hoppers to Tyne Dock in 1968. (Kind courtesy of Roy Lambeth, not to be reused)

Above and below: A pair of Class 24 diesels heading to Tyne Dock with a rake of loaded iron ore wagons. (S. V. Walton)

Above and below: These two images show a Class 24 diesel on the iron ore train banked by a pair of Class 17 Clayton diesels. Claytons were trialled on the iron ore trains but were not a success. (Kind courtesy of Bill Watson, not to be reused)

The route from Tyne Dock for iron ore changed in the 1960s when the line between Boldon colliery and Washington was closed, and the iron ore went via Gateshead and down the East Coast Mainline before coming onto the line at Ouston junction. By the 1970s, most of the traffic for the line came via Ouston junction, with some trains continuing on the original S&TR route to Washington where the Leamside line was joined. By then, traffic to and from the steel works formed most of the traffic, and was the reason for the line staying open, with most of its coal coming from east by rail. The 56-ton hoppers went out of service following a change in equipment and route from 1974. The iron ore now came into Redcar as the port could handle larger ships, and 100-ton hopper wagons were used, again in rakes of nine, pulled by two Class 37s. With the closures of the other lines serving Consett (south towards Bishop Auckland cut in 1939, north to Newcastle via Rowlands Gill on the Derwent Valley in 1963, and the Lanchester Valley in 1966), the goods station at Blackhill was served by a shunter from Consett. The history and services on the Tyne Dock to Consett line in the post-war era are covered in great detail on the South Pelaw Junction website southpelawjunction.co.uk for those seeking further information on this era.

A shunt of coal wagons at Annfield Plain resulted in disaster on 9 December 1964. Twenty-three wagons got away, running down the gradient for several miles and striking the rear of a goods train near Beamish, killing the guard, CY Ridpath of Sunderland. The driver, T. Waller, was taken to Durham County Hospital with shock but the fireman, G. Milley, was uninjured.[2] Another train from Morrison Busty colliery was involved in an accident in 1970 when, hauled by a Class 37 diesel locomotive on its way to Dunston, the diesel derailed at Ouston junction where the line joins the East Coast Mainline. The guard was in the rear cab of the locomotive and jumped when he saw the wagons derail,

A tanker train heading between Annfield Plain and Leadgate, hauled by a Class 37. (S. V. Walton)

Iron ore train at the tippler at Consett, 1973. (Beamish Museum)

being killed by the wagons which were piling up. Traffic for the P&SSR was re-routed via Washington, and East Coast Mainline trains via the Leamside line, until the accident was cleared and track repaired.

Morrison Busty colliery at Annfield Plain was in operation until 1973. Access to the pithead was via Annfield East junction onto the original S&TR line, following it eastward over Oxhill crossing but then leaving the original route after reversing to head westward to the colliery. After its closure, traffic on the line focused on the steelworks at Consett. This came to an end in 1980 with the closure of the works which the town of Consett was built on and relied on as its main source of employment, as well as the wider economy. The closure came as a huge blow and meant there was no reason for the railway to continue in operation. Special passenger trains were run, including those involving the Derwentside Rail Action Group who mounted a campaign to get British Rail to reinstate passenger services on the line. Unfortunately, this did not occur, and the final train was run on 17 March 1984. It was originally intended to be a Diesel Multiple Unit, but owing to the large amount of interest, Class 46 diesel No. 46046 *Leicestershire & Derbyshire Yeomanry* hauled a rake of Mk 1 carriages from Newcastle Central station to the site of Consett station (with steps used to allow people onto the snowy ground), and later returned to Newcastle.

Following this, the only trains run were scrap trains, lifting the line and ever reducing the line's length until Ouston Junction was reached. A short section of the line is in use still for freight, from Brockley Whins northwards before branching off for the site of Tyne Dock, now Port of Tyne, and further north a section is also used for the Metro service, with the new interchange with the bus service meaning it now stops short of crossing King Street. A new Metro training depot is on the site of the old wagon works, with the northern limit of surviving S&TR trackbed featuring a portacabin and picnic table as a rest area. Much of the route, joining at Washington and taking the 1893 and 1886 deviation lines, forms part of Sustrans c2c cycle path from Sunderland to Whitehaven, continuing on the western half of the S&TR line to branch off at Parkhead. Many under and overbridges remain, together with other fine engineering works including the Beamish cutting and numerous embankments. Forty years on, there are now calls to reopen a line to Consett, possibly using this trackbed, owing to the rise in population in the area and congestion on the roads, a story echoed many times over elsewhere in the country.

The final passenger train on the line on 17 March 1984, with Stanley in the background. (Beamish Museum)

Class 08 diesel shunter 08217 at Consett shortly after the ironworks closed. (Brian Page)

Notes

Chapter 1

1. *Newcastle Journal*, 15 September 1832.
2. *Durham Chronicle*, 13 January 1837.
3. *Durham Chronicle*, 24 November 1837.
4. *Newcastle Journal*, 22 September 1838.
5. *The Globe*, 11 May 1833.
6. *Durham County Advertiser*, 24 January 1834.
7. *Durham Chronicle*, 28 March 1834.
8. *Newcastle Courant*, 18 May 1834.
9. *Newcastle Journal*, 13 September 1834.
10. *Newcastle Journal*, 4 November 1837.
11. *The Shields Daily Gazette*, 25 July 1899.

Chapter 2

1. *Newcastle Evening Chronicle*, 26 June 1939.
2. Beaumont, R., *The Railway King – A Biography of George Hudson, Railway Pioneer and Fraudster* (Headline: London, 2002).
3. *Morning Herald*, 4 November 1848.

Chapter 3

1. *Newcastle Guardian and Tyne Mercury*, 22 September 1855.
2. *Morning Herald*, 26 April 1856.
3. Addyman, J. F., *North Eastern Railway Engine Sheds* (Cramlington: North Eastern Railway Association, 2020), p. 170.
4. *Yorkshire Gazette*, 14 August 1858.

5. *Durham Chronicle*, 31 December 1858.
6. *Newcastle Courant*, 30 April 1858.
7. *Richmond & Ripon Chronicle*, 11 December 1858.
8. *Shields Daily Gazette*, 26 March 1859.
9. *The Sun*, 26 September 1861.
10. *Morning Herald*, 27 September 1861.
11. *Morning Herald*, 25 October 1862.
12. Report made by Captain Tyler, R. E. to the Board of Trade regarding the explosion of the boiler of a mineral engine at the Stella Gill station of the North Eastern Railway, 31 October 1861, www.railwaysarchive.co.uk.
13. Hewison, C. H., *Locomotive Boiler Explosions* (Newton Abbot: David & Charles, 1983), pp. 62–63.
14. *Durham Chronicle*, 21 August 1868.
15. *Northern Echo*, 3 March 1874.

Chapter 4

1. *Morpeth Herald*, 3 February 1894.
2. *Daily Gazette for Middlesbrough*, 17 August 1896.
3. *Northern Echo*, 21 February 1896.
4. *Durham County Advertiser*, 9 April 1897.
5. *Shields Daily Gazette*, 8 October 1896.
6. *Morpeth Herald*, 29 September 1900.
7. *Yorkshire Post and Leeds Intelligencer*, 11 December 1900.
8. *Newcastle Evening Chronicle*, 8 August 1901.
9. *Newcastle Evening Chronicle*, 30 September 1902.
10. *Newcastle Daily Chronicle*, 29 September 1903.
11. *Durham County Advertiser*, 1 April 1904.
12. *Durham County Advertiser*, 11 November 1904.
13. *Newcastle Evening Chronicle*, 10 August 1905.
14. *Newcastle Evening Chronicle*, 14 December 1905.
15. *Shields Daily News*, 23 April 1906.
16. *Newcastle Daily Chronicle*, 25 April 1906.
17. *Newcastle Evening Chronicle*, 31 July 1906.
18. *Newcastle Evening Chronicle*, 28 December 1906.
19. *Shields Daily News*, 29 December 1906.
20. *London Daily News*, 3 August 1907.
21. *Yorkshire Evening Post*, 3 August 1907.
22. *Newcastle Evening Chronicle*, 6 August 1907.
23. *Newcastle Evening Chronicle*, 3 June 1908.
24. *Newcastle Evening Chronicle*, 18 August 1910.
25. *Newcastle Daily Chronicle*, 27 September 1912.
26. *Newcastle Evening Chronicle*, 1 July 1914.
27. *Hartlepool Northern Daily Mail*, 29 January 1913.

28. *Newcastle Evening Chronicle,* 12 February 1913.
29. *Newcastle Journal,* 23 February 1914.
30. *Newcastle Evening Chronicle,* 30 August 1915.
31. *Consett Guardian,* 13 August 1915.
32. *Newcastle Journal,* 20 January 1917.
33. *Newcastle Journal,* 21 February 1917.
34. *Newcastle Daily Chronicle,* 21 November 1918.

Chapter 5

1. *Durham County Advertiser,* 13 December 1901.

Chapter 6

1. *Shields Daily News,* 15 July 1925.
2. *Newcastle Journal,* 29 August 1927.
3. *Newcastle Evening Chronicle,* 21 January 1939.

Chapter 7

1. *Newcastle Journal,* 12 April 1969.
2. *Liverpool Echo,* 10 December 1964.

Bibliography

Archival

Beamish Museum
Photographic Archive

Head of Steam, Darlington Railway Museum Ken Hoole Study Centre
Ken Hoole Photographs & Documents collection
RH Inness notebooks

The National Archives
AN 13 British Transport Commission
RAIL 390 London & North Eastern Railway
RAIL 569 Pontop & South Shields Railway Company
RAIL 663 Stanhope & Tyne Rail-Road Company
RAIL 1021 T. E. Harrison

Published

Addyman, J. F., *North Eastern Railway Engine Sheds* (Cramlington: North Eastern Railway Association, 2020)

Atkinson, F., *Industrial Archaeology of North-East England Volume 1* (Newton Abbot: David & Charles, 1974)

Atkinson, F., *Industrial Archaeology of North-East England Volume 2: The Sites* (Newton Abbot: David & Charles, 1974)

Ayer, T., *Annfield Plain In Old Picture Postcards* (Netherlands: European Library, 1989)

Baldwin, J. H., 'The Stanhope and Tyne Railway; a study in business failure' in *Early Railways: A Selection of Papers from the First International Railway Conference*, edited by Andy Guy and Jim Rees (London: Newcomen Society, 2001) pp. 325–341

Beaumont, R., *The Railway King – A Biography of George Hudson, Railway Pioneer and Fraudster* (Headline: London, 2002)

Crump, N., *By Rail to Victory – The Story of the LNER in Wartime* (London & North Eastern Railway: Norwich, 1947)

Darsley, R., *Consett to South Shields via Beamish* (Midhurst: Middleton Press, 2009 (2016))

Donnelly, J., *South Pelaw Junction*, www.southpelawjunction.co.uk

Harrison, C. A., 'Self-Acting Inclines' in *The Railway Magazine* (December 1898)

Harrison, F. E., 'The Pontop Inclines' in *The North Eastern Railway Magazine* (February and March 1923)

Hodgson, G. B., *The Borough of South Shields: From the Earliest Period to the Close of the Nineteenth Century* (Newcastle: Andrew Reid & Co., 1903)

Hoole, K., *A Regional History of the Railways of Great Britain Volume 4: The North East* (Newton Abbot: David & Charles, 1965 (1978))

Hoole, K., *North Eastern Locomotive Sheds* (Newton Abbot: David & Charles, 1972)

Mountford, C. E., *Rope & Chain Haulage: The Forgotten Element of Railway History* (Melton Mowbray: The Industrial Railway Society, 2013)

Mountford, C. E., and Holroyde, D., *Industrial Railways and Locomotives of County Durham Part 1* (Melton Mowbray: Industrial Railway Society, 2006)

Rolt, L. T. C., *George and Robert Stephenson: The Railway Revolution* (London: Longmans, 1960)

Rounthwaite, T. E., *The Railways of Weardale* (Railway Correspondence and Travel Society, 1965)

Tomlinson, W. W., *The North Eastern Railway, its Rise and Development* (Newcastle: Andrew Reid, 1914)

Warren, K., *Consett Iron 1840 to 1980, A Study in Industrial Location* (Oxford: Clarendon Press, 1990)

Whishaw, F., *Railways of Great Britain and Ireland Practically Described and Illustrated* (London: John Weale, 1842)

Whittle, G., *The Railways of Consett and North-West Durham* (Newton Abbot: David & Charles, 1971)

Woods, N., *A Practical Treatise on Railroads* (London: Longman, Orme, Brown, Green, 1838)